Smart Love Solutions for School-Age Children and Teens

Also by Martha Heineman Pieper, Ph.D.
and William J. Pieper, M.D.

Smart Love

Smart Love Solutions in Early Childhood

Addicted to Unhappiness

Smart Love Solutions for School-Age Children and Teens

A Handbook for Parents, Teachers, and Caregivers

Martha Heineman Pieper, Ph.D.
William J. Pieper, M.D.

Published by Smart Love Family Services

SMART LOVE®
FAMILY SERVICES

Smart Love Family Services
Smart Love Preschool
800 W. Buena Ave
Chicago, Illinois 60613
p: 773.665.8052
f: 773.525.4097
contact@smartlovefamily.org
www.smartlovefamily.org
www.smartlovepreschool.org

Smart Love Solutions for School-Age Children and Teens

ISBN: 978-0-9826790-1-2

The greatest improvement in the quality of human life
will come not from brilliant discoveries about the nature of
matter or technological innovations, but from parents
whose love and insight give their children lasting inner happiness
and thereby leave a legacy of competent, caring individuals.

–Martha Heineman Pieper, Ph.D., & William J. Pieper, M.D.
Smart Love

Contents

Foreward

It is a pleasure to bring you this new and expanded volume of Smart Love solutions to common questions about how best to respond to school-age children and teens. The Smart Love approach was developed by child development experts and parents of five, Martha Heineman Pieper, Ph.D., and William J. Pieper, M.D. *Smart Love* helps parents raise happy children who over time come to regulate their own behavior within a deeply satisfying parent-child relationship. Endorsed by child development experts here and abroad, *Smart Love* is a unique, evidence-informed approach to parenting and child development.

The non-profit Smart Love Family Services opened its doors soon after *Smart Love* was published. We offer a range of services such as: child development classes, counseling, parent coaching, and training and consultation in the *Smart Love* approach to other agencies. We recently added The Natalie G. Heineman Smart Love Preschool to our "family" of services. The Preschool provides a play-based curriculum for children ages 3, 4, and 5 as well as programs for infants and toddlers with their parents or caregivers.

Our hope is that *Smart Love Solutions for School-Age Children and Teens* will guide parents, teachers, and caregivers both in the home and in the classroom to guide happy, healthy and successful children and teens.

Carolyn Stolper Friedman
Executive Director
Smart Love Family Services and
the Natalie G. Heineman Smart Love Preschool

Introduction

For years parents have asked us their most pressing parenting questions, and we have responded to them in our monthly *Smart Love* column in *Chicago Parent*. This handbook represents all of the questions we have answered about preteens and teens.

We are psychotherapists, consultants to other mental health professionals, and parents of five children. Our work with unhappy and difficult children, our experience with children who were thriving, and our ongoing parenting responsibilities combined to show us how vital it is for children to see themselves as loving and lovable. This work also led us to a new understanding of the goals of childhood and how to best help children attain them.

With the benefit of this large pool of experience, we developed the concepts that fill *Smart Love*. Initially, we set forth our conclusions about child development and mental illness in *Intrapsychic Humanism*, a text written expressly for professionals and academics. As word about *Intrapsychic Humanism* began to spread within the professional and academic worlds, we were repeatedly asked if we would write a book specifically for parents. That decision was the genesis of our book, *Smart Love: The Compassionate Alternative to Discipline that Will Make You a Better Parent and Your Child a Better Person* (Harvard Common Press, 1999). We have since published a self-help book geared toward adults called, *Addicted to Unhappiness: Free Yourself from Moods and Behaviors that Undermine Relationships, Work, and the Life You Want* (McGraw Hill, 2003).

In *Smart Love*, we have collected practical guidelines that will enable parents to give their children the specific kind of love they need to grow into happy, fulfilled adults. We've seen the effectiveness of our unique approach with children, adolescents, and parents from all walks of life and different racial, ethnic, economic, and cultural backgrounds.

Smart Love will guide you to help your child make constructive choices in the context of an ongoing close relationship. If you use these guidelines, your child will come to recognize that the deepest happiness results from loving and feeling lovable and loved, rather than from satisfying particular desires or achieving specific goals. Your child will learn to govern her/himself better through the desire to feel happier and more competent than s/he ever would from fear of negative consequences.

Smart Love teaches you how to best satisfy your child's developmental needs and how best to manage her immature behaviors. With the guidelines we provide, you can help your child acquire a stable inner well-being that is unaffected by success, failure, or other ups and downs of daily life; and that will enable your child to reach her/his full potential.

Parents and professionals alike often ask us about other parenting approaches that advocate using discipline or permissiveness to guide their children. *Smart Love* is unique because it replaces both of those methods with what we call *loving regulation.* Loving regulation means you stop the child from doing whatever behavior you think is inappropriate at that moment, but you maintain closeness with them, and you don't impose any unpleasant consequences. The point isn't just to get kids to do what you say, but also to try to help them learn to make good choices. That's what loving regulation is all about. You stay positive with your child. What the child learns is that they may not be able to have the thing they want at a given moment, but they can always have a close relationship with you. That's why loving regulation actually produces children who are the opposite of spoiled, because material things do not assume such incredible importance to them. They can always fall back on a close relationship with you.

We have learned that if you put the time in at the crucial moments of development when kids really need the time, then your job as parents will be easier as the child grows older because your child is going to be autonomous and happy. Kids who are unhappy consume an enormous amount of adult time. The good news is that at any point in a child's life, we can help them become happier people. If parents have gotten bad advice and been overly harsh with children, it's never too late to change that.

Smart Love is based on the most current research about child development. It is the first parenting approach that helps you see the world through your child's eyes at each stage of development. It helps you see your children as children, which will help you relax and enjoy them. This takes the worry out of parenting. It tells people what to expect and what to do. We're offering parents a really different approach to being parents that we think is so much more enjoyable and will produce happier and more responsible children.

This year we are taking the *Smart Love* philosophy into the classroom and opening Smart Love Preschool in Chicago. Our hope with this new endeavor and the publication of *Smart Love Solutions For School-Age Children and Teens* is that our children have as many enjoyable hours as possible, whether inside the classroom, at home, or out in the world.

About the Authors

Martha Heineman Pieper, Ph.D., and William J. Pieper, M.D., are co-authors of numerous articles and books, including *Intrapsychic Humanism: An Introduction to a Comprehensive Psychology and Philosophy of Mind* (Falcon II Press, 1990); *Smart Love: The Compassionate Alternative to Discipline that Will Make You a Better Parent and Your Child a Better Person* (Harvard Common Press, 1999, 2001), and *Addicted to Unhappiness: Free Yourself from Moods and Behaviors that Undermine Relationships, Work, and the Life Your Want* (McGraw-Hill, 2002, 2004). The Piepers also wrote a monthly column, *Smart Love,* for *Chicago Parent.* They have conducted numerous workshops for professionals and parents, and Martha Heineman Pieper has made appearances on Fox TV, NBC TV, and numerous talk radio shows. For over thirty years they have conducted clinical research and been in private practice treating children, adolescents, and adults; counseling parents; and supervising other mental health professionals.

Martha Heineman Pieper graduated Phi Beta Kappa and Magna Cum Laude from Radcliffe College, and received her Ph.D. in clinical social work from the University of Chicago. She has served on the editorial boards of professional journals such as *Illinois Child Welfare, Social Work* and *Smith College Studies in Social Work.* In addition to her clinical writings she has published extensively on the topic of philosophy of research. She is on the Board of Directors of Smart Love Family Services and the Intrapsychic Humanism Society.

William J. Pieper received his B.S. and M.D. degrees from the University of Illinois. He completed residencies in adult psychiatry at the University of Illinois Neuropsychiatric Institute in Chicago, and in child and adolescent psychiatry at the Institute for Juvenile Research in Chicago. In 1975, he graduated from the Chicago Institute for Psychoanalysis with certificates in child and adult psychoanalysis.

He has taught at the University of Chicago School of Social Service Administration and in the Institute for Psychoanalysis adult and child psychotherapy programs. He is on the Board of Directors of the Intrapsychic Humanism Society.

Chapter One
School-Age Children

Introducing long-absent father to his nine-year-old son

Q I am a twenty-five-year-old single mother of three children, ages nine, six and four. I was married to an extremely abusive man for six years. It's been two years, without a cent of child support. The man refuses to work. He is the biological father of the two younger children. But my oldest child has a father who is more than willing to pay his part.

Here's the problem: My ex-husband was so controlling he would not allow me to accept money from the father of my first child or allow him to see the child. Now eight years later, I am able to collect child support and allow the father of my first child to see him. How do I tell my child about his real father coming into the picture? He's a stranger. What can I do to facilitate a healthy relationship between the two?

A Most important is to give your son the news in a positive manner. You might say something like, "I have really exciting news. Your Dad is going to be coming to see you now. He has wanted to see you for a long time but it wasn't possible, and now it is. He has also always wanted to contribute money to support you and now he can do that as well."

Then take your cue from your son. He might respond in a number of different ways. Perhaps he will be overjoyed, in which case you can just agree that this is a happy moment in his life. Or perhaps he has coped with his father's absence by convincing himself that he neither misses him nor wants to see him. In that case, he might make a comment such as, "Well I don't want to see him. He should just stay away." If your son is negative about the reunion, show him that you understand his feelings while at the same time encouraging him to give his Dad a chance. You could say, "I know you feel angry that he hasn't been a part of your life and he has missed out on so many important moments, but it's so important to try to keep in mind that your Dad always wanted to be part of your life. I think you will feel happiest if you try your best to give both of you the opportunity to get to know one another." Your son may have many reactions to his first meeting with his Dad. For example, he may have constructed an image of a father that is larger than life and he may feel disappointed when he first meets the real flesh-and-blood man. In that case, you might point out to him that his relationship with his father has been imaginary for so long that the reality will inevitably feel a little strange and take some getting used to.

Most important is to allow your son to share both positive and negative feelings and to accept his negative feelings while at the same time you gently steer him in the direction of keeping an open mind about the relationship. In counseling his father about the first meetings, do suggest activities that your son particularly likes and help his Dad to understand that it may take time before the boy actually accepts him as his father. Finally, you will need to be very sensitive to the reactions of your other two children, who may feel jealous and bitterly disappointed that their older brother has a caring, responsible father. Helping them with these feelings may require a lot of patience and understanding, but you will make a real contribution to their emotional well-being if you can sympathize with their loss. Also, once your older son's father has established a relationship with him, you might ask if he could find it in his heart occasionally to spend some time with the other two children as well. Including them once in a while in an outing with their older brother might help take the edge off their resentment.

Protecting your child's feelings from daddy's emotional distance

Q I now you have answered a lot of questions about divorced families, but our situation is a little different. My ex-husband has remarried and has two new children. My ex never asks to have our 8-year-old daughter, he never keeps most of his scheduled visitations and he doesn't ever want her at Christmas. It seems as though his new family has wiped our daughter from his mind. She often asks why her father doesn't come for the visits and around Christmas she asks if she will be invited to spend time with him. When I tell her "no," she becomes very depressed. I have tried calling my ex to tell him that he is really hurting our daughter's feelings, and he says he will make more effort, but nothing really changes. I know this is very painful for my daughter, but I don't know what more I can do. Suggestions?

A It is terribly sad when parents divorce their children as well as their spouses. No child could understand that a father (or mother) is unwilling to see her because the child is associated with a failed marriage. Children always and understandably feel there is something undesirable and unattractive about them that is keeping the parent from wanting to be with them. Given the depression your daughter is exhibiting, we think it might be advisable to seek the opinion of a mental health professional to see if your daughter might benefit from some psychotherapy. In the mean time, please emphasize to her that she is a wonderful child who deserves a father who would want to spend time with her and that you hope at some point her father will come to his senses. If you have men friends who would enjoy joining the two of you on outings and showering some positive attention on your daughter, that might help as well.

Is it OK if a child prefers to spend time alone?

Q My daughter is the most solitary person I have ever met. She seems completely content being by herself. This has been the case since she was about three years old (she's nine now) and I always thought she would discover an interest in friends as she grew older. But now, when her peers are increasingly involved in their social lives, to the point that some of their moms are concerned they are too into them, my daughter still has very little interest in spending time with others.

In all other ways she is a sweet, happy kid. The other kids don't dislike her, but I think they leave her alone because she doesn't reach out to them. Should we be concerned? Are there other things we should watch for?

A You say your daughter is a "sweet and happy kid," but you don't say how she occupies herself. If in addition to seeming happy she is doing well in school and keeping busy with interests and hobbies (reading, music, computer games, etc.), we would advise you not to worry about her.

Don't forget that your daughter spends most of the day at school surrounded by other children, so it's not the case that she is having no social life at all. That said, there is no harm in diplomatically asking if she would like to invite a friend the next time you are going to a movie or a museum.

On the other hand, if your daughter spends a lot of time just sitting and not doing much of anything, something may be bothering her. Try to engage her in enjoyable activities and gently ask her how her day at school was, how her studies are going, how she is getting along with the other children. Think about whether there are stresses or upsetting events at home that might be worrying her and, if so, talk to her about them and then try to shield her from them if possible.

Emotionally dependent daughter

Q My eight-year-old daughter (her brother is ten, her sister is six) is very smart, very creative, and very emotionally dependent on me. Unlike her siblings, she never plays alone; when she's not with a friend, she's interacting with me or moping around the house complaining of being bored. She's also going through a phobic stage the last six to eight months. At least six times a day, she checks in with me, worried about marker fumes she may have inhaled, or paint that might have gotten into her mouth, or a disease she might have. I should add that, in this emotional profile, she mirrors me. Although I have more self-awareness and have developed coping mechanisms, we're two peas from the same pod. Any words of wisdom?

A It sounds to us as though as the middle child your daughter is feeling the need for extra attention. The most helpful response to her "emotional dependence" is to fill her tank by giving her as much positive attention as you can spare. If possible, spend some time with her every day in an activity of her choosing. If she says she is bored, perhaps you could involve her in a project (cleaning, cooking, filing papers, etc.) with you. If you include her in your work whenever possible, you will be satisfying her need to be with you and creating opportunities for pleasurable chats.

We believe that your daughter's phobias are, at bottom, a result of her need to have more of your attention. All children are convinced that "to be like is to be liked." Unconsciously, your daughter believes that if she is like you in every way, including sharing your fears, you will want to spend more time with her.

If you both reassure your daughter each time she comes to you and also give her as much of your time as possible, her phobic behavior may decrease. It might also reassure her if you tell her that you had many of the same fears at her age and share with her some of the coping mechanisms you have developed.

Desperate for attention

Q My eight-and-a-half year old daughter is an energetic and bright girl, but she's also very exhausting. She always wants to be performing or have somebody entertaining her. She's wearing me out. But whenever I try to talk to her about how she needs to let me and other people have some time to ourselves, she seems to tune me out. In fact, any time I try to talk to her gently about anything about her behavior, she seems to think I'm "lecturing" her and I can see in her eyes that she isn't listening. I know this is a big topic, but can you advise me on how to begin to approach it? Thank you so very much!

A We suggest that you begin by accepting that, for whatever reason, your daughter is feeling uncertain of your positive feelings for her and, in turn, is feeling somewhat negatively about herself. This inner discomfort is the reason that she needs so much attention. She constantly seeks your attention as a way of trying to reassure herself that you care for her and want her to be happy. The reason she "tunes out" when you lecture her is that no matter how gentle you feel you are being, she experiences your negative comments as signifying that she is a bad person. This meaning is so painful that she has to try to wall it off.

Once you realize how insecure your daughter is feeling, you may find it easier to offer her the ongoing reassurance she so badly needs. Try not to push her away or make her feel ashamed of needing you. If you are able to offer her generous amounts of time and positive attention at this critical time, you will help build her confidence and her belief in your positive regard for her. This inner well-being will, in turn, make her less desperate for your constant attention.

Occasional bedwetting

Q I was intrigued by your reference to bedwetting as a deeper emotional issue. My almost seven-year-old daughter has struggled with this for the past several years. After toilet training shortly after turning two, she required diapers at night for many years. From age five to seven, we have experienced months of dry nights and then periods of bedwetting of several nights in a row. Her level of food and liquid intake is not significantly different to account for these periods of relapse. I must add that she is a middle child and not as forthcoming with her feelings as I would like. I would appreciate your advice in this matter.

A If your daughter is only wetting the bed a few nights every several months, it seems clear that the wetting is caused by tensions left over from her daily life. If she has mentioned problems at school or with friends around the time of a recurrence of bedwetting, you might suggest gently that perhaps the strain she is feeling during the day is carrying over into the night. Also ask yourself whether you have been feeling stressed out and have perhaps been more critical than usual. If so, you might share with your daughter that you have been feeling under pressure yourself and didn't mean to take it out on her.

In the months when your daughter is not wetting, do try to help her to realize that you are a resource for sharing information about herself and her feelings. In that way, you can establish yourself as someone she can turn to for help with stressful situations.

If at family times she is being overshadowed by her younger and older siblings, try to make some time alone with her every day—at bedtime or during chores such as grocery shopping or walking the dog. If something is bothering her, be sure that you give her plenty of room to express her frustration, anger or sadness without immediately trying to "fix" the problem yourself. In other words, rather than saying, "Why don't you just [take this action]," say something like, "I can understand that what happened could be very upsetting. What are your thoughts about how to respond?"

As your daughter experiences you as a good listener and a source of comfort, she will be more likely to come to you and less likely to wet the bed during periods that are especially difficult for her.

Loss of a father

Q My husband passed away in May. My children miss him terribly (my daughter is six and my son is 3½) and often cry. My daughter tells me she often speaks to him in her dreams and sees him while we are walking. Is this her way of mourning, or should I see a psychotherapist aside from her counseling, which she attends one time per week?

A At the moment, your daughter seems to be handling the loss as well as can be expected. She seems to have accepted the tragic fact of her father's death and to be mourning it in an age-appropriate manner. These vivid moments of re-experiencing her father may persist for many more months and, even, years, and they will fade only gradually.

One indication that your daughter is working hard to face this painful reality is that she talks with her father only in her dreams and does not think he is really present in her waking life. Dreams are times when we rewrite reality the way we want it to be. No wonder your daughter dreams her father is back with her again! It is also not surprising that your daughter believes she catches glimpses of her father. Adults as well as children have the experience of thinking that they see an absent loved one in a crowd.

The good news is that your daughter is sharing her mourning process with you, thereby giving you a wonderful opportunity to help her grieve. Young children believe they are all-powerful, and your daughter may feel that she did something to make her father want to leave. Times when she tells you she dreams about him or sees him are golden chances to emphasize that her daddy did not want to abandon her and that sometimes even parents can't make things turn out as they want.

We know you must be struggling with your own feelings of grief just as your daughter is struggling with hers. Do share with her how much you miss her father and your knowledge that it will take a long time for that pain to ease. The strong bond you have with your children will help all of you to get through this painful and difficult process.

Dividing a single mom's attention

Q I am a single mother of two children, ages ten and six. My daughter (age ten) has a lot of homework this year. Sometimes she needs help but mostly she just wants me to be with her while she completes it. But my son (six) also wants attention and this causes a lot of tension. If I play with him or read to him, it distracts my daughter. But if we go in another room, she feels abandoned. This is made more complicated by my having the kids weekdays (when my daughter has homework) and their father having them weekends (when they can relax and have fun). I don't know how to handle this, how to give each child the attention they need when they need such different kinds at the same time. Can you offer any advice?

A As we are sure you know, one of the difficult parts of being a single mom with two children is that you are outnumbered, with the result that frequently there is not enough of you to go around. Moreover, given the inevitable feelings of sadness and loss children feel when their parents divorce, your children are probably especially in need of your attention at this time.

We suggest that when your children arrive home from school you sit down with them and plan out the evening. Ask your daughter what homework she will need help with. Ask your son if he would prefer that you work with your daughter first and play with him later, or vice versa. If you involve your children in decisions about how the evening will go and how your attention will be shared, they will feel more in control of satisfying their needs for your time and attention. You might even consider making an evening schedule and posting it on the refrigerator.

It is understandable that since your daughter doesn't see you on weekends, she wants to be in your presence even at times when she is autonomously doing her homework. You have obviously succeeded in establishing a warm relationship with both of your children, and they value their time with you very highly. So when you are playing with your son, make clear that every fifteen minutes or so you are going to take a break to visit your daughter, give her a hug, and ask her how things are going. The knowledge that she is not isolated from you for long periods of time should help your daughter to work independently and to avoid the distraction of being in the same room with you and her brother. Also, given the difference in your children's ages, perhaps after your son goes to bed and your daughter has finished her homework, you will have some time before her bedtime to chat with her.

When you are talking with your daughter or helping her with homework, try to think of ways to keep your son happy and busy. Perhaps he likes stories on tape, art projects or electronic games. Once he realizes that there is a plan for the evening that ensures that both he and his sister will have your attention, he probably will be more relaxed when you have to spend time with your daughter.

Once in a while, take the opportunity to mention to the children that although you and their Daddy believe that getting divorced was the right thing to do, you know it is hard on them and that they wish their Daddy could be with them on school nights and that you could be there on the weekends. The knowledge that you are sympathetic to the loss they feel will help your children to share their feelings about the divorce. This in turn will make them more secure and not so anxious about getting enough of your attention.

Kids who refuse to eat

Q Help, please. I have a nephew (age ten) and niece (age nine) who are the victims caught in the process of a painful divorce. My brother is living at home again and currently has partial custody of his children. When the kids are over at my parents'/brother's home, they refuse to eat. My mother and/or brother try to fix their favorite meals, but even then they complain it is not cooked correctly when it is fine. All these mealtime battles have become a very tense and unpleasant situation each time they are over.

My nephew in particular is the main problem. He has even gone so far as to tell my brother (his dad) that he has decided to hate his grandmother (our mom) since my brother hates his mom. There is a lot of hostility and control issues. But, at what point do you draw the line and force the kids to eat?

P.S. If they don't eat dinner at my parent's house, they will get junk food and snacks later at their own mom's house.

A To answer your specific question, you never want to force children to eat because even if you succeed (and it's more difficult than you would think), you will scar them emotionally. In any event, the real issue is not food, but the bitter divorce between the children's parents and the way the entire family is getting drawn into the conflict.

If the children don't feel comfortable eating at their dad's house, the reason is not that they are being willful. Most likely, they feel that to eat their dad's (or their grandmother's) food is to take sides against their mother. So they try to wait until they get back to their mom's house to satisfy their hunger.

In other words, where they eat has become a loyalty test, and they obviously believe they have to take sides like every one else in the family. When their father and grandmother pressure them to eat, they experience them as asking them to be loyal to their father and disloyal to their mother and they resist even more vigorously.

The only genuine solution to this problem is for the adults in the situation to begin acting with the children's interest in mind. This means that everyone involved should avoid saying anything negative about either parent in the children's presence. It would help if the children's mother and father could sit down with them and apologize for the strife that has been so upsetting to them. The parents need to make it clear that although they no longer want to live together, they love their children and will do everything in their power to avoid making the children feel that they have to take sides.

If the parents and other relatives are able to respect the children's natural wish to remain close to both parents and not to hear anything negative about them, the children will no longer feel that where they eat is a test of their loyalty. At that point, they will be willing to eat at their father's house as well as at their mother's house.

Encouraging young children to care for their teeth

Q My 6-year-old refuses to brush his teeth. We have tried everything from bribery to taking away favorite foods, but nothing works. He doesn't really give a reason except that he "hates" to do it. He has already had cavities in his baby teeth and his dentist says he has to brush at least once a day. We are truly at our wits' end. Please advise.

A Tooth-brushing has become a power struggle between you and your son. This is the first problem that must be addressed. Sometimes, making tooth-brushing a joint effort is all that is needed to solve this problem. Tell your son that you are going to brush your teeth and ask if he would like to brush alongside you in the bathroom.

Another approach is to take him to the drugstore and let him pick out the toothbrush and toothpaste of his choice. Then, see if he would like to start by "brushing" one of his toys or bath animals. The goal is to engage his interest and sense of fun so that he doesn't feel he is losing a battle when he brushes his teeth. If you take this approach, we feel certain his reluctance will fade.

How do I combat my child's excessive sweet tooth?

Q What is the best way to restrict candy and sweets? My eight-year-old has a real sweet tooth, but she also has three fillings. Fortunately, they were in her baby teeth, but the dentist is concerned that if she doesn't change her eating habits, her permanent teeth will be affected. The dentist says she can have chocolate once in a while if she brushes her teeth immediately afterward.

My daughter is very upset. Today when I was cleaning out her backpack, I found lots of empty candy wrappers. When I confronted her, she said she got the candy from friends at school who felt sorry for her.

I scolded her, but I am still worried that she will beg candy from her friends (and hide the wrappers next time.) Suggestions?

A The problem with scolding is that it can teach children to cover up behavior they know you won't like.

Forming an alliance with a child is the most effective

way to change behavior. Sit down with your daughter and review the dentist's advice, including brushing, flossing and the restriction on sweets. Explain that she will have her permanent teeth for the rest of her life and that she needs to take care of them. Ask her what kind of sweets schedule she can live with. Suggest that she eat the allotted chocolate at home when her toothbrush is available. If you solicit her input and make sure she feels the plan is doable, she will feel she owns it and not that it is being imposed.

Encourage her to tell you when she slips and has extra candy by promising to rethink the schedule if it proves too difficult. Once your daughter feels she can share problems with you, you will be in a much better position to help her with solutions in other areas of her life as well as in this one.

Irrational fears

Q My seven-year-old daughter recently began refusing to be upstairs if the rest of us were downstairs, and vice versa. When she wants something on the other floor, she insists that someone has to come with her, claiming she's "afraid." She doesn't really seem scared, and I'm getting impatient with this behavior. What's going on here, and how should I handle it?

A Clearly, something is making your daughter feel uncomfortable when she is by herself. You don't say whether there have been major changes in your family, but stressful events can leave a child feeling unprotected. Or maybe you have been gone more than usual and your daughter is reacting to your absence. If nothing within your family seems different, you might ask your daughter in a gentle, concerned way whether she has had a traumatic experience of some kind outside of the house, such as being frightened by a stranger, or seeing a violent TV show at a friend's home.

Regardless of the reason for your daughter's intense need to be in your presence, try to respond with acceptance and compassion. Your child is not manipulating you, and she is not faking unhappiness. She is feeling real inner turmoil, and it is healthy for her to turn to your relationship for soothing. Even though she is seven, you remain her most important source of comfort and strength and your willingness to respond positively when she needs you is a crucial component of her sense of self-worth.

If you aren't supportive of your daughter's need for your help, she will have to find less constructive ways to ease her anxiety, which could include an incapacitating fear of leaving the house, nervous habits, difficulties in school, or recurrent nightmares. Moreover, since she copies the way you treat her, if you are unsympathetic now, later, she may have trouble turning to others when she is upset and comforting those close to her when they are distraught. On the other hand, if you respond positively to your daughter now, you will head off more serious symptoms, and you will help her grow into a woman who has a reservoir of inner well-being that will enable her to become a caring, loving adult who will help others when they need her.

I'm worried about how we can calm my son's fears

Q My eight-year-old son has been increasingly asking questions whenever his dad or I aren't at home. Questions such as: "Is Mommy OK?" "When is she coming home?" "How long is Daddy working?" Or when it's bedtime for him and his brother: "Are you going to bed, too?" Some days I can answer his questions calmly. Other days I want to scream. Where are these worries coming from? He doesn't like being separated from the family at any time and is very overprotective of his baby sister. How can I help him calm down? He's too young to have all these concerns.

A Usually, when children have excessive fears about members of the family, either they have experienced a traumatic event, such as the death or serious illness of a close friend or relative and are concerned that tragedy will strike again, or they have angry feelings that they worry are so powerful that they will harm those close to them.

If no one in your son's life has been seriously ill or injured, then perhaps you need to consider whether his fears result from angry feelings he is not comfortable acknowledging. Children tend to have very unrealistic beliefs in the power of their feelings – they really believe angry thoughts can kill. It sounds as though your son is feeling resentful over the arrival of a new baby and perhaps because you don't have as much time to spend with him. He may be checking on everyone's well-being to make certain that the family is safe from his angry reactions.

We suggest that you talk to him about the fact that it is normal to feel upset or angry sometimes, especially when a baby joins the household and draws everyone's time and attention. Invite him to share these feelings with you any time. Also, be sure you are making enough special time to spend with your son so as to reduce any feelings he may have of being pushed out of the limelight by his baby sister.

What do I do when my daughter is teased?

Q My 8-year-old daughter had a harelip, which was surgically corrected, but she is left with a speech defect. Her speech therapist feels that eventually she will have normal speech. In the meantime, though, other children tease her and imitate her to the point that she refuses to talk in class. Now she doesn't want to go to school. She is a very bright child and has always enjoyed school. I don't think she should be in a special education class, but I don't know how to help her regain her confidence. I have tried telling her that she should ignore the other children and then they will stop, but she says they hurt her feelings and she can't ignore them. Please advise.

A In situations where children with disabilities are teased, we have found that it is often very effective to have teachers lead discussions with the aim of raising sensitivity about disabilities and how to respond to those who have them. One teacher got the class to think about how much courage it took for a boy with a withered arm to come to class and try to keep up with the children with normal builds. She had everyone in the class put one arm behind his or her back and try to go through the school day that way. She found that after this exercise, the children stopped teasing the boy and went out of their way to help him. If your daughter's teacher would be willing to do some sensitivity training, your daughter may begin to have a more positive school experience.

The odd girl out

Q My third-grade daughter has been part of a threesome with two other girls for the past two years. Though they're chummy and often get along very well, there are too many times when one or another of the girls is "on the outs," shunned by the other two. This leads to many tears and cries of, "I have no friends," "Nobody likes me," and "I hate them." They're in the same class again this year. Can you offer any advice?

A When children are having a hard time with their friends, parents will be most helpful if they focus on the one part of the problem they can affect positively – their own child.

In other words, rather than trying to help your daughter change her friends, aim to help her cope constructively with the ups and downs that characterize elementary school friendships.

When your daughter comes home upset because she is the odd girl out, show her that you know this is painful, but suggest that there is a better solution than once again trying to break into an exclusive twosome and being rebuffed. Help her learn to walk away from an unrewarding relationship experience by finding other children who might be receptive to playing with her. You might even offer to take her and a friend or two bowling, to a movie, or out to dinner. As has happened over the last two years, her two best friends will inevitably get tired of being exclusive and invite her to rejoin them.

Your daughter's unhappiness with her friends is a wonderful opportunity to help her learn one of life's most important lessons – that the purpose of friendship is mutual enjoyment and respect and that it is neither necessary nor desirable to cling to a friendship that has turned abusive.

How to handle kids' friends

Q I try to practice a gentle parenting style with my seven-year-old son, but I never know how to handle it when he has a friend over and they get into an argument or start doing things we don't allow in our house—things that are either unsafe or destructive. When I try to reason with them or gently encourage them to stop, it doesn't really work, and I end up resorting to threats, like if they don't stop, the friend will have to go home and I'll call his parents. What do you suggest?

A When children repeat problematic behaviors, the best solution is to engage in some advance planning. If you employ this strategy, you will avoid the unpleasantness of threats and enable your son to enjoy socializing with his friend. We suggest that you not invite the friend over unless you have the time to come up with a constructive, fun activity and to help see it through. For example, seven-year-olds often enjoy cooking lunch or arranging chutes for falling marbles. For the time being, the best solution might be to take the boys outside the house to a setting that allows them more freedom, such as a playground or a children's museum.

If you follow these guidelines, you will achieve your goals of keeping your son happy and safe, helping him socialize appropriately, and protecting your house, while you also maintain a close and positive relationship with your son.

What do I do with my son's inappropriate birthday gifts?

Q My 8-year-old son just had a birthday party. We took 14 boys bowling and had a great time. The problem is the presents he got, which include DVDs and a video game we would never let him see or play. My son wants to see them because they were gifts, and his friends will ask if he liked them. I hate to spoil his good feelings, but I can't see letting him do things that we would not allow just because his friends gave them to him.

A No parent likes to take away a child's present, yet you don't want to abandon your principles. We suggest you offer to put away the movies and video games until your son is old enough to watch and play with them. Then, let your son choose acceptable replacements. Your son will have more presents in the end, and you will feel comfortable with what he is watching and playing.

Should my eight-year-old be prepared for the worst?

Q My eight-year-old daughter has a classmate who was just diagnosed with brain cancer. She will have to have surgery, chemotherapy, radiation, and the prognosis is uncertain. My daughter announced her friend's illness to us very casually—"Samantha has a cancer in her brain; the doctors are going to take it out." It is clear my daughter has no idea of the severity of Samantha's illness. I am wondering if I should tell her in advance that her friend may not get better so that she will be prepared for bad news if it comes. But I also wouldn't want her to tell her friend that I said she might die. What do you suggest?

A Actually, the best way to protect your daughter is not to give her additional information. Children do best when they assimilate bad news at their own pace. Like other eight-year-olds, your daughter probably doesn't hesitate to ask questions about anything and everything. If she is not following up her announcement about her friend's illness with questions, it is because she is not ready to hear more. Your best approach is to stand by and wait until your daughter asks for more facts. You can also watch for changes in your daughter's moods or behavior, which might be caused by her unconscious reaction to this loss. If you see signs such as irritability, trouble sleeping, bad dreams, etc., ask her if something is bothering her. If she doesn't know, gently ask, "Maybe you are upset about Samantha?" Perhaps she will pick up on your suggestion and talk about her feelings. If not, at least you will have planted the notion that her friend's illness might be affecting her in ways she doesn't realize.

Meanwhile, you might suggest that she make a get-well card or go with you to buy a book or something else that will amuse her friend during her treatments and hospital stay. Helping your daughter take an active, caregiving role will allow her to feel less powerless in the face of her friend's illness.

Build on interests to reignite love of reading

Q My 8-year-old is having a tough time with school. He hates homework and puts it off as long as possible. Once he has done it, he doesn't want anything to do with reading or being read to, which he used to enjoy. He says, "Yuck," if I suggest he read on his own and rejects offers to read to him even at bedtime. I am worried this lack of interest in reading will harm him in the long run, but I don't know what to do. All he wants to do is play computer and video games and watch TV. The only healthy thing he does is to play baseball with his friends when the weather is good. Can you help?

A It is not unusual for children who are being introduced to homework to react negatively to having their free time interfered with. Parents can soften the blow by sympathizing with their children's resentment, making themselves available to answer questions or just offering to sit with their children while they work.

You are right to worry because your son seems to have generalized his dislike of homework to reading and being read to. He seems to have identified reading with work, and TV and electronic games with fun. The best way to make elective reading fun is to build on your son's interests. Since he likes baseball, go to the library and choose some action books that have baseball as their subject. Additionally, look for books that match other interests he might have, such as pets or other sports.

If you haven't already done so, limit the amount of time your son can spend watching TV and playing video games, so he has the opportunity to try some of the books you have selected. You might also buy some games that involve reading or words and offer to play them with him. Another idea is to get him some audio books he can listen to on a portable device.

How do I help my star student get back on track?

Q My 8-year-old daughter just started third grade and is struggling. She seemed to be doing OK in first and second grades, but suddenly she is having trouble keeping up in math, science and history. She says the teachers don't explain things well, but then we get notes from the teachers saying she isn't handling her homework.

This is affecting how she feels about herself–she calls herself "one of the stupid kids," and says she hates school. I am inclined to help her, but my husband says he always heard it is bad for parents to work with children, that children transfer their natural rebelliousness to learning situations and won't do what parents say. What do you advise?

A When young children who have been doing well in school suddenly begin to struggle, a common explanation is that they need glasses, are having hearing problems or have another physical ailment. Get her a complete physical.

If she gets a clean bill of health, think about whether other worries are affecting her ability to concentrate – a problem in the marriage, illness in the family, a new sibling or some other major disruption. If so, help her to share her feelings about these things so she isn't trying to cope on her own.

If the root problem turns out to be school related, meet with her teachers to figure out what is happening and enlist their help. Sometimes 8- and 9-year-olds feel self-conscious about asking questions in class because they don't want to appear "stupid" in the eyes of their classmates. They leave class without really understanding the material and then have difficulty completing the homework, which leaves them even further behind.

If this is the trouble, the teachers can encourage her to ask questions and make sure she understands the lesson. You can help your daughter understand that being smart doesn't mean knowing everything, but rather means knowing what you don't know and getting the help you need.

Finally, if you can work with your daughter in a positive way without becoming upset when she doesn't know an answer, by all means help her with her schoolwork. Working with you will help her develop the confidence she lacks right now. If it turns out that your sessions with her turn into conflicts, ask her teachers to suggest a tutor or find a tutoring center in your area. There is every reason to think that with your support your daughter can get back on the track academically.

Hostility to schoolwork

Q According to his teacher, my fifth grader is not working to his potential. We know that he puts off doing his homework and then rushes through it. We have tried holding back his allowance and restricting him from activities, but that didn't work. In fact he became very sulky. My friends suggest offering him rewards like renting a video he likes. What do you think would help?

A First we suggest that neither punishments nor rewards will solve the real problem, which is that for some reason your son is not enjoying the learning experience. Punishing him only made him dislike his studies more. If you entice him with rewards, he may work for the reward, but that will not introduce him to the pleasure of learning. When the rewards cease, his motivation will run out of steam.

The best long-term solution is to find a way to help your son enjoy his studies. The first step is to show him that you are on his side. Ask him how he feels about school—which subjects he likes, and which subjects are causing him trouble. Then ask what you can do to help. Perhaps he would like to have a tutor who would help him with the subjects with which he is struggling.

One strategy we have found effective is to invite him to be in the same room with you when he is doing his homework, so that he will have an adult available to answer questions as they arise. Because your goal is to show him that learning can be fun, do your very best to be positive and never negative when answering his questions. For example, if he has made a mistake, rather than telling him he has done something wrong, tell him he made a good try. Rather than just giving him the answer, show him how to divide the question into small steps that will lead to an answer.

The best way to discover that learning can be fun is to share the problem-solving effort with someone who is positive and enthusiastic. If you can be that person for your son, or you can find a tutor who offers these qualities, your son's natural curiosity will be stimulated and he will begin to get more enjoyment from his studies.

Refusal to Accept Blame

Q My six- and ten-year-old sons both have a problem accepting responsibility for their actions. The six-year-old simply will claim "someone or something" made him do it; or he'll tell a "little white lie" (e.g., "Josh wanted me to have a bite of his pizza.

He said I could," as Josh sits there in tears.) My ten-year-old is more self-righteous. He always thinks he is being unfairly blamed and wants a chance to tell his side of the story. We are trying to model good examples of accepting blame when we do things wrong. Why is this so difficult for our boys, and is there anything else we can do to help them?

A Like many other parents, without realizing it, you are expecting too much of your children too soon. Because their self-esteem depends to some extent on their ability to get what they want when they want it, all children bend the truth at times. Not until adulthood can children consistently maintain their inner equilibrium when they cannot have their heart's desire. So when your six-year-old wants a piece of pizza, it is normal for him to eat it if he can get it and then rearrange reality ("Josh wanted me to have it") to justify his actions. Similarly, your ten-year-old still needs to bend the truth occasionally in an attempt to make the world conform to his wishes. When he sees that you do not understand this need, he feels unfairly blamed.

Forcing children to accept "blame" at those times when they need to bend the truth is both ineffective and harmful. Because they love and adore their parents, parental disapproval causes children a great deal of unnecessary pain. In an attempt to avoid this pain, children are driven to become better liars. Being children, they do need to distort reality at times, so they respond to unpleasant consequences by trying to do a better job of hiding their tracks.

The best response to the child who has broken a rule and covered it up is to help him understand why he needed to distort reality and to show him that he doesn't need to hide the truth from you. If your six-year-old ate his brother's pizza, say something like, "Obviously that pizza looked so good, it was really hard to resist it even though it belonged to someone else." The next time, get enough pizza for everyone, or suggest to the ten-year-old that he not leave it around where his little brother can get it.

If you can respond understandingly to your children's normal urges to make reality conform to their wishes, you will help your children to feel understood and to understand themselves, and you will reduce their need to conceal their actions from you in the future. In other words, punishing children for bending the truth simply makes them into better liars, whereas showing them understanding and compassion will help them develop into reliable truth-tellers.

Battles over piano practice

Q My seven-year-old has been taking piano lessons since he was four. He has never liked practicing, but recently practicing has turned into a really unpleasant battle. He puts it off as long as possible and then we have to tell him that he can't watch a video or do other things he likes if he doesn't practice. That only seems to make him hate it more.

Now he's saying he wants to quit piano altogether. I would allow this for the sake of peace in the house, but I hate to see him lose all the ground he has gained. His playing is just beginning to sound decent. What do you advise?

A This is not a battle you need to be fighting! You are treating piano lessons as though they were school—that is, as though they were something your son has to do. In reality, playing a musical instrument, like taking basketball or ballet, is purely for fun. If it's not enjoyable for your son, there is no reason why he should continue.

So let him stop if he wants to. Think about how upset you would be if someone told you that you had to do an activity you hated in your free time. If you are matter of fact about his stopping and don't make him feel ashamed or guilty, you will make it possible for him to return to the piano at a later date if he changes his mind.

Chronic nail-biting

Q My nine-year-old daughter bites her nails. My wife and I haven't had to cut them for years, so you get some idea of how continuous this is. She's generally a happy, self-confident child. My wife says this is just her being an oral person. (She also sucked her thumb until she was six.) I am worried that it's her way of handling stress, but not sure if it's a good or bad way. Sometimes when she's playing outfield, I notice she seems more focused on her nails than the game, for example. And it just doesn't seem like a great idea to be nibbling on her nails. It seems like a good way to expose herself to more germs. What do you think? And if it is a bad habit, what can we do about it?

A We think that your wife is probably correct that your daughter's habit of thumb-sucking became transformed into the more socially acceptable habit of biting her nails. As with all nervous habits, the more you focus on her nail-biting, the more anxious and self-conscious she will be about it, and the more she will be likely to do it. As for germs, just encourage her to wash her hands when they get dirty.

Nail-biting is a sign of stress. Even though your daughter seems happy and self-confident, perhaps she has some worries she feels hesitant to share with you. Try asking her in a relaxed way how things are going at school and with her friends. Also think about her time at home. Are you able to spend some enjoyable, unpressured time with her, or are most of your interactions focused on things she must accomplish, such as chores or homework? If you can find ways to help her share her social or academic concerns and also, to the extent possible, relieve her of the pressure of external demands, over time your daughter will feel more relaxed, and the nail-biting will decrease.

Nail-biting gifted child

Q My nine-year-old son has been biting his fingernails for four years. He chews not only his fingernails, but also the skin on his fingers. He has chewed them so severely that I fear his fingernails will never grow back normally again. We have tried spraying "Bitter Apples" on his fingers so they will taste bad. We have not done this consistently. I am concerned that if I could get him to stop biting his nails with this method, he might substitute some other bad habit instead.

He may grow out of this at some point, but I would like to help him before his fingernails are permanently deformed. He wet the bed until age seven. We used the bell and pad device successfully. He has had encopresis for the last four years which has greatly improved. He is an only child and gifted. Do you have any suggestions how we can help him stop biting his nails?

A Actually, the question is not how to help your son stop biting his nails but how to help him feel sufficiently happy and confident that he doesn't need nervous outlets to get through the day. The bed wetting, encopresis and nail-biting are expressions of anxiety and a lack of inner security.

Focusing on the nail- biting will make your son feel more pressured and anxious and make it harder for him to stop biting his nails. Even if you succeed in inhibiting the nail biting, your son is likely to develop another symptom to relieve his inner tension. As an only child, your son is naturally the focus of many of your hopes, wishes, and fears. Moreover, as a gifted child, your son may feel that he must always succeed and perform well. This can be a heavy burden to bear.

We suggest that you start by stepping back and reexamining your day-to-day expectations for your son. Does he have some down-time every day to spend doing whatever he likes? Do you keep in mind that he is a child so that you feel comfortable when he makes mistakes, hesitates, or doesn't feel like working? Are you expecting him to be more grown-up than his age warrants?

Remember that despite your son's precocity, he, like all children, needs lots of love, hugs and positive comments. Clearly, you are deeply devoted to your son. If you can focus for a while on taking the pressure off him and surrounding him with love and affection, you will help relieve your son of inner tensions that can only be soothed by nail-biting or other symptoms.

Witnessing other parents being harsh

Q This is a question about how, as parents, we can and should react to the way other parents are treating their children. Too often I am in the grocery store and see a parent yell at or even slap their child. It pains me and I want to say something, but I don't want to make anything worse for the child by making the parent angrier.

Any suggestions how parents can say the right thing in a situation like this and help encourage angry parents not to treat their kids this way? Or is there no point and we just have to learn to turn away? Thank you.

A This is a tough and, unfortunately, all too common situation. If the parent is clearly emotionally or physically abusive, you should find the nearest policeman or call 911 or the DCFS abuse hotline. If, on the other hand, the parent is behaving harshly without crossing the line into abusiveness, there is probably not much you can do. If you comment on the parent's behavior, you may make the parent angrier at the child and cause the parent to be even more cruel to the child when they are alone.

This is why it is so crucial that both expectant parents and new parents be helped to understand how vulnerable their children are to their anger and disapproval, and be given constructive ways to manage any anger they may experience in their children's presence.

How to help kids resist peer pressure to break safety rules

Q My nine-year-old son loves to skateboard with his friends after school, but I worry because when he is with them he doesn't wear a helmet or pads even though that is our rule. He says his friends think it is "stupid" to wear protective gear and he doesn't want to be teased for being different. I can understand his point of view, but I don't want him to hurt himself. What do you recommend?

A This is a wonderful opportunity to help your son to understand that his health and safety are more important than his friends' approval and that there are times when he needs to "just say no."

You might begin by talking about the nature of true friendship. Real friends would not give him a hard time for following the rules you have set and for wanting to protect himself. Then emphasize that if staying in the good graces of his friends means putting himself at risk, the price of that friendship is too high because no friendship is more important than his physical safety.

Ideally, your son will respond to your discussion by gaining the strength to tell his friends that he is going to wear the protective gear and to ignore any teasing that results. If he still feels unable to say "no" to his friends, we suggest that you ask your son how you can be of help. Perhaps for a while you need to be physically present when he is skateboarding with his friends so that he can say he "has to" wear protective gear in order to skate. Or he may think of other ways to use your authority as a buffer between him and his friends, such as telling them that you are going to drop in randomly to check on him or that he doesn't feel he can break his promise to you.

It is critical, though, that you do not accept the premise that it is OK for him to skate unprotected in order to keep the peace with his friends. Your insistence on this point will both keep him safe now, and also will make it easier for him later on if friends try to convince him to smoke, take drugs, or engage in any of the other dangerous activities that are available to preteens and teens.

My daughter hates school and she's only in first grade

Q My six-year-old daughter started first grade this fall and she has been coming home saying she hates school. At first she refused to talk about it, but I gently persisted and she finally said that she is the "worst" at math, that all the other kids know their addition and subtraction and she doesn't. They have something called a "math minute" in which they have a minute to see how many addition and subtraction problems they can do. She says other kids get scores of more than twenty out of twenty-five, but she almost never gets more than six or seven. I have tried to reassure her by telling her that first grade is the place to learn math, but she says everyone else already knows it. I feel really badly for her, but I don't know what to do to help. I never knew that children had to know math by first grade. What do you suggest?

A We have heard this kind of understandable frustration from many parents who discover too late that there are schools that expect children to enter first grade with both reading and math skills. Many kindergartens do not believe in teaching math and reading to five-year-olds, which is fine. Rather than realizing that with instruction they can catch up, many children measure themselves against their peers and conclude that the problem is that they are not smart enough. These children often respond by disliking reading, math and school. In this way, children like your daughter are needlessly being discouraged and made to feel inadequate.

Talk to your daughter's school and see if they offer after-school help or other enrichment programs to enable your daughter to catch up in math. At home, you can think of fun ways to practice addition and subtraction. If you have a computer, there are many math programs for first graders that children find enjoyable. Most important is to continue to tell your daughter that the problem is that she wasn't taught math in kindergarten, not that she can't learn it, and that you are totally confident that she has the talent to become an excellent math student.

How do I get my kids to stop their squabbling?

Q I have two girls, ages eight and ten. All they seem to do is pick on each other. They argue about everything, including which TV programs to watch, who hogs the bathroom more and who has better friends. They also call each other names and take each other's things. Their quarrels end in tears and they run to me, each one trying to convince me she is right. I have little patience for this and I usually send both of them to their rooms. But the moment they are released, the fighting starts again. What do you suggest?

A Your children have become comfortable with conflict and negativity and they turn to those negative experiences out of habit or when they are bored. Because this pattern of interacting has been going on for a long time, it will be hard to change, but with persistence, you can succeed.

Your goal is to help your girls realize they will feel much happier if they can relate to each other positively rather than negatively. Unfortunately, simply telling them this will not have much effect. You need to make it possible for them to experience the superior pleasure of closeness and friendship. There are a number of strategies you can try and only trial and error will tell you which are most effective.

First, make sure each of your girls is getting some time alone with you doing something she likes. Often children snipe at each other because they see each other as rivals for their parents' attention.

Then, see if you can think of activities in which a goal can be reached best by cooperating. For example, take them kite flying, where one person runs with the kite and the other holds the string. Or ask them to help you prepare a meal where each person makes a different dish.

Another strategy is to recognize boredom as it is setting in and head off conflict by having a store of things the girls like to do—anything from art projects to bike riding—when possible.

Finally, for things that must be shared, such as the TV, bathroom or telephone, buy a big kitchen timer. When the timer sounds, time is up and it's the other girl's turn.

Remember that while progress may be slow, like all people, if given the chance, your girls will ultimately prefer closeness to conflict.

Sick of squabbling

Q Is sibling rivalry inevitable? My three kids (ages nine, seven, and four) argue about everything. I can't get the nine-year-old to set a better example for her brothers, or get the seven-year-old to realize that his little brother can't be expected to understand all the picky details of the games he creates and tries to play with him.

I feel like there's always arguing in my house, and it wears me out. I know this is a bigger problem, but I just want to know whether I should just resign myself to all the arguing and let them work this out on their own more, or I should tell them that when something causes such disagreement, they have to stop playing it and do something else. (I do try to take one aside for one-on-one time as often as I can, but then the other two get into arguments. I don't call these fights because they really aren't. They're just loud conversations that involve an awful lot of "No!" and "You're doing it wrong!" and "Stop it!" Sometimes I even wonder if it bothers me more than them!)

A Sibling rivalry is inevitable only in the sense that siblings who are out of sorts (hungry, overtired or ill) will frequently take their discomfort out on each other in the form of squabbling. Sibling fighting becomes a cause for concern only if siblings regularly hurt each other physically or devastate each other emotionally, or if they never have friendly moments.

It sounds as though your children are in the squabbling category because their fighting takes the form of bickering and they seem to want to play together. There are, however, steps you can take to reduce conflict and help them to take pleasure in each other's company.

First, even though it is tempting to expect your older children to behave in a parental manner toward the younger ones, siding with the younger children by telling the older ones to be more understanding or responsible nearly always backfires. The older children (who are still children, after all) are bickering because they feel out of sorts or at their wit's end. They need to be cared for, so they really don't have it in them to be patient and understanding at that moment. Moreover, when older children are made to feel responsible for squabbles, their resentment of their younger siblings increases and they become more angry and less friendly toward them.

Second, try to find some non-competitive activities your children would enjoy. If they are engaged in play that doesn't pit them against each other, their time together will be more harmonious. Examples are fishing, bike-riding, planting a garden, painting, cooking, or being read to.

Finally, do your best to ignore squabbling that remains "harmless" and relatively contained. If it starts to escalate, don't assign blame, but tell all the children in a neutral way that if they can't get along when they are doing something together, you will help them to find an activity they can do by themselves. You will be pleasantly surprised at how often your children will choose to cooperate so as not to miss out on the fun of playing together.

Aggression toward an older sister

Q I have two children, one is a ten-year-old female and the other is a seven-year-old male. I need help! My daughter at times is loving and nurturing with her brother and at other times is the sister from the "black lagoon." This is especially so when she is with her friends. My son reacts by lashing out at her physically.

His behavior is now changing at school. He has physically hit another child that, as he says, always bothers him. I have spoken to both of my children, given timeouts, taken away favorite things and grounded them. Nothing is working! Help!

A If your son is hitting both his sister and also children at school it means he is frequently finding himself at the end of his rope emotionally. Hard on your son as your daughter may be at times, it is unlikely that her actions are causing his aggressive behavior. You may want to consider whether there are significant stresses in his life or in yours that are making him anxious and upset.

Your daughter sounds like a fairly typical sibling—loving and nurturing at times, and annoying at other times, especially when her friends are around.

You don't say what your son does when your daughter and her friends are together; if he is insisting that they include him in their activities, it is not surprising that he is being rebuffed. When your daughter has friends over, we suggest that you help your son find constructive alternatives to the vicious cycle of bothering his sister, being rejected, and striking back. Either invite a friend for your son, spend some special time with him yourself, or find an activity that he will enjoy doing.

Most important, try not to respond to your children with disciplinary measures, such as time-outs and grounding. Although you intend these punishments to persuade your children to be nicer to each other, unfortunately they will have the opposite effect. Because your children adore you and want to be just like you, they will copy your responses and become even harsher toward each other.

Instead of discipline, we recommend that you use the Smart Love approach of loving regulation. When you use loving regulation, you manage your children's behavior effectively without attaching unpleasant consequences, which are counterproductive.

Loving regulation teaches children to be kind to themselves and others. When your daughter and son provoke each other, simply step in and tell your children in a friendly manner that they must be civil to each other or they will have to play separately. If your daughter has friends over, help your son disengage and find another activity.

Loving regulation will teach your children that disagreements can be handled in a caring manner. This lesson will carry over to your son's experience with his classmates and make him less inclined to hit back when he feels frustrated or put upon.

When to intervene

Q To what extent should I let my kids argue? I hear them raise their voices at each other and hurt one another's feelings by saying things I'd never say to them, like, "You're such a baby" when one of them cries, or "Get out of my room," or "I don't want to play with you." They are both boys, ages seven and nine. It feels like they are doing to one another everything I try not to do to them.

A Unless the boys come to you for help or are physically hurting each other, you can safely assume that it is better to let them work out their differences together. What we would advise, though, is that you take these squabbles as a sign that the boys need more positive input from you. If you can make time each day to spend alone with each boy, even as little as twenty minutes, they may see each other less as competitors and more as friends.

Or maybe they are squabbling because they are bored, hungry, or tired. If their wrangling continues for more than a few minutes, have some enjoyable activities in mind that the three of you could do together. For example, the boys might like to help you make dinner or they might like an opportunity to go outside with you and play ball, run and climb, or walk the dog. By responding in this way, you will not only make their day more pleasant, but you will also show them that constructive fun is much better than the diversion of bickering with each other.

How do we get our daughter into her own bed?

Q How do I handle my seven-year-old daughter who still sleeps with us? She has a lot of fear about sleeping in her own bed. My son, who is now fourteen, also slept with us until he was seven. When my daughter was born, he was moved out to make room for her. Help!

A The move a child must make to sleeping in her own bed is the difficult part of co-sleeping. It's important to transition gradually. If the choice were left to them, most children would stay in the parental bedroom until adolescence. You also need to be aware that, unlike your son, who could see that he had to make way for the new baby, your daughter is neither prepared for the change nor desires it.

Your strategy, therefore, should be gentle and gradual. Have family time in your room before your daughter heads to her own bedroom. This will make clear that your daughter is not being abruptly exiled. Read a book, listen to music or talk for fifteen or twenty minutes. Then walk your daughter to her room and spend some quiet time there.

If she is afraid for you to leave, you may have to put in extra time the first few nights—perhaps even sleep on the floor. Don't sleep in her bed. You want her to sleep by herself. If you have a family pet, perhaps it could keep her company.

Think of things to make her room as enjoyable as possible, such as a tape recorder, new doll or stuffed animal. If the problem persists, you can try two-way radios so she can communicate with you from her room. With your patient help, your daughter will become comfortable in her own bed.

How do I respond to my eight-year-old's fear of being alone at night?

Q My eight-year-old daughter has become fearful about going to bed in her own room at nght. This came on kind of suddenly. She's always wanted a night light on and her door open, but lately she comes out several times after we put her to bed and says things like, "Can't I sleep with you in your room?" We really can't think of what has changed in her life to make her feel insecure about sleeping alone.

We don't want her in our room with us, but we feel kind of bad about saying, "No, you're a big girl and you need to sleep in your own bed." We also wonder how much we should do to help her settle in for the night after we've read stories, sung lullabies and tucked her in. Should we come back and rub her back again and again until she is asleep? Or must she learn to fall asleep on her own? This is eating up what little time we have to ourselves in the evening, and although we feel like maybe that's selfish, we also need some time of our own at night! Thank you.

A Have you tried asking your daughter if something is bothering her? When a child suddenly becomes anxious and fearful, odds are that something in her life is newly stressful. Perhaps she is upset about something at school. For example, maybe she is having trouble with friends, difficulties in a subject, or one of her teachers is being critical.

Try to create moments of "togetherness" when she can tell you about her school and social life. Next, consider whether there are family worries or tensions that might be affecting her. Even if you can't come up with a "reason" for her fears, do assume that they are very real to her. So do your best to be responsive and understanding. Help her stay in her room by rubbing her back or sitting with her. If you have things to do, tell her that you will be back in fifteen minutes to check on her (and be sure to come back on time and to keep coming back as long as she needs you). As time goes by, if you can maintain your patience and caring, your daughter will get over this anxiety. Coming down hard on her and forcing her to be alone when she is frightened will intensify and prolong her fears and make her feel isolated from you. So follow your good instincts and help her through this difficult phase.

Misspelled notes show sincerity, not stupidity

Q My eight-year-old just had a birthday and she has been writing thank-you notes for the presents she received.

My question is what to do about all the spelling and grammatical errors she makes. I don't want her to look bad by being compared to other kids who spell and write better, but if I correct her writing it seems somehow not honest.

She hates to be corrected and gets really mad when I tell her to rewrite something. What do you recommend?

A It is terrific that your daughter is happy to write her thank-you notes without putting up a fuss. You really don't want to interfere with her graciousness by making her feel inadequate about her writing.

We suggest you either help her with spelling and grammar at some other time, or, better yet, if she doesn't like being corrected by you, leave the instruction to her teachers.

You don't have to worry that she will "look bad" if there are mistakes in her note. The recipients will be delighted to have their gifts acknowledged and will have only the most positive feelings about your daughter. Any errors will assure them that the notes are authentic and not dictated by you.

How Can We Make Our Boys More Gracious?

Q With the holidays coming, we are again facing the question of how to get our boys ages 2, 4, and 6 to say appropriate thank you's for the presents they get from their relatives. Some presents come from far away and require some sort of note. Others are given to them in person. Usually, they dive into the presents and give a perfunctory "thank you" when pressured, but I don't think the relatives who have gone to all the trouble to choose and wrap gifts feel properly appreciated. The note writing is even worse, all we hear is, "Later." My husband and I feel the children are taking present-getting for granted. How do we get them to be more gracious?

A First of all, it's important to differentiate among your children in terms of age. It is too much to expect a 2-year-old to take a break from looking at a new toy to say a "proper" thank you. You can try saying, "Can you say 'thank you' to Aunt Anne?" as your 2-year-old is ripping the present from its wrapping. But if no response is forthcoming, tell Aunt Anne what a wonderful choice she made and how much your son will enjoy it. The 4- and 6-year-olds are more able to say thank you reliably, but, again, their focus will be on the present rather than on expressions of gratitude. One strategy is to wait until they have played with the new toy for a while, at which point they may have more emotional space to give heart-felt thanks. Again, if they fall a little short, fill in for them by remarking how much use they will get from the gift and what an inspired choice it was. As for the notes, we suggest that you make printed thank-you cards with each child's name on them. Then the child can "write" his name and/or draw a picture, which will seem easier and more fun than facing a blank page. The goal is not to make the child feel inadequate or criticized because he isn't old enough to engage in adult-style gratitude, but to praise him for his age-appropriate efforts.

The value of commitments

Q My eight-year-old daughter, like many of her peers, is involved in too many activities, but she likes them all. They're a nice mix of activities: art, music lessons, Brownies, soccer and Sunday School (in addition, of course, to school). She's been asking me to sign her up for gymnastics too, but I've always felt that would put all of us over the top.

Here's the rub: After a wonderful soccer season, she was asked by her coach to join the traveling team, which is more intense, practices more often and travels to more distant games. The coach is wonderful and her teammates are great, but it's taking over all of our lives already, and he plans to increase practices to three or four times weekly next year.

My daughter says she'd prefer to quit soccer altogether rather than do that. I asked whether she would consider returning to the other league, since she loves soccer and this is her only team sport. She says no, she'd rather try something new, like gymnastics. I feel sad to see her drop soccer altogether. She loves it and gets a lot out of it, socially and physically, and I much prefer the soccer culture to that of gymnastics.

So here's my question: When should a parent encourage a child to stay with something in which she has invested so much (and which she likes) and when should a parent just chalk it up to having been a good experience and let her move on?

A This is a question that nearly every parent confronts at some point. The basic guideline is that after-school activities are for recreation—that is, for fun. Children have so many things they must do, including seven to eight hours of school plus homework. It is crucial not to turn their recreational time into a chore as well. Even though your daughter has become very proficient in soccer, if it has ceased to appeal to her, don't override her wish to make a change.

Your daughter sounds like a child with broad interests who will go through a sorting-out period until she settles on an activity that she wants to pursue intensively. If you force her to stick with soccer, it will cease to be fun and will become something she does for you rather than for herself. On the other hand, if you are accepting of her decision to change activities, you teach her the all-important lesson that recreation adds balance to life by providing periods of pure enjoyment. If you are uncomfortable with gymnastics, try to find another activity with which you and your daughter are both comfortable.

Parents are often told that their children should be made to stick with activities they have started in order to learn lessons about the value of making a commitment. But this is really not a moral issue. Adults do not pursue recreational activities that have ceased to be fun and there is no reason to apply a different standard to children.

Is A 7-Year-Old Ready To Get An Allowance?

Q Our 7-year-old has recently begun asking for an allowance, saying all her friends get them. My husband thinks she ought to work for it since he had to when he was a child. He thinks the allowance should be contingent on whether or not she does her chores. He worries giving our daughter money will not teach her the value of a dollar. I see his point, but I know this approach will lead to conflict. I dread it and think we should avoid the allowance issue altogether.

A In our opinion, the best approach to allowances is to make them a treat and allow children to spend or save as they wish. Making them conditional on behavior or chores will bring conflict. Unconditional allowances does not spoil children any more than clothing or feeding them makes them believe they won't have to work as adults.

Childhood is a period of normal dependency and it is parents' responsibility to gratify their child's needs, including the need for some discretionary spending money. We believe this type of allowance will actually make her happy and confident and teach her to be generous to others. Moreover, having a little money to spend or save at her discretion will provide her with a nearly opportunity to weigh the relative merits of immediate spending on small items vs. saving for more significant purchases.

Should I accuse my son of stealing?

Q My seven-year-old came home from school with a GameBoy he said he "found" lying on the ground. I am suspicious of his story, but he swore it was really true.

I don't know whether to accept his story or to check with the school. If I believe him but he stole the GameBoy, I feel like I will be encouraging him to steal again. If I challenge him by calling the school, I'm afraid he won't feel trustworthy. What do you advise? And if I do call the school and find that he stole it, what should I do then?

A You don't have to accuse your son of lying to check with the school. Tell him that before you can let him keep the GameBoy you need to call the school to make sure no one lost it. If no one reported it missing, there is no reason not to let him keep it. However, if someone did report the GameBoy missing, you should go with your son to school to make sure it is returned. If you then discover the GameBoy was not dropped but was taken from a locker, you will need to talk with your son.

In your discussion, keep in mind that nearly all children take something that doesn't belong to them at some point—only a tiny fraction grow up to steal as adults.

The object is not to make your son feel like a criminal. That would only drive him to cover his tracks better in the future. The next time he may not tell you he has "found" something of value. Rather, show your son he can get things he wants in ways that do not hurt others. For example, you might tell him that if he wants a GameBoy, he can save his allowance and you will add the money necessary to buy it on his next birthday or on the next big holiday.

Most important, emphasize you are proud of your son for telling you that he had the GameBoy and making it possible for you to help him to do the right thing and return it. Suggest that the next time he feels he really wants something other children have, he should talk to you and you will help him make a plan.

Should I force my child to go to summer camp?

Q I have enrolled my first-grader in day camp for the first eight weeks of the summer. I didn't ask him, because I assumed he would want to go. When I mentioned it to him, he said he absolutely did not want to go. He has a three-year-old sister and I didn't think it would be much fun for him to spend the summer with her and me. I think it would be much better for him to be with his friends at camp. But he seems very adamant about this. I have tried offering him things he wants, like a scooter, but he continues to refuse. I hate to move on to threats or removing privileges, but that's about the only other thing I can see to do. Can you suggest a way to get him to go?

A There is no reason to pressure your son to do something that is really quite optional and recreational. Since you are available to be with him, there is no compelling reason he has to go to day camp.

If you make clear that it is his choice and then ask him to keep an open mind and try camp for a day or two with the understanding that if he doesn't like it he doesn't have to go, he may soften his negative stance. Perhaps your son is feeling that his sister is getting all of your attention while he is at school and he feels that going to camp will continue to deprive him of your company. You could suggest that after camp you will be sure to spend some "special time" with him. If your son remains adamant about not wanting to attend camp, perhaps he would like some focused activities that require less of a time commitment, such as art, music, or sports lessons a few times a week. If all else fails, you will have the opportunity to spend a lot of time enjoying your son this summer.

Insecurity about being a short boy

Q My eight-year-old son is a head shorter than the other children in his class. He feels self-conscious about it. Normally a quiet kid, at his last pediatrician's appointment, he asked the doctor to give him pills to help him grow. The doctor told him, "You don't need pills to help you grow. You need to learn to like yourself for who you are," and then he turned to me and said, "And you need to help him."

How can I help my son feel good about his size when so many societal messages stress that tall is better? And how can I help him deal with the teasing he gets when other kids call him "shorty" or "pip squeak?" What can I do as a mother to help my child like himself?

While I know the doctor is right—my son has to learn to like himself for who he is—I often wish like him, that I could just give him a magic pill to help him grow. I see how sad this makes him and I feel helpless and responsible. After all, it is my and my husband's genes.

A We all wish that our children could go through life without experiencing the pain of being teased by other children, but children are rarely, if ever, that fortunate. Most children have some attribute that becomes the focus of teasing. These attributes can range from wearing glasses, to having braces, to being overweight, to being underweight, to having an accent, to being poor, to being short.

The best help for a child who is being teased is to explain that the children who are teasing him are unhappy inside and mistakenly believe they will feel better if they can get other children to feel equally unhappy.

Tell your child that no matter how hurt he feels, if he can manage to ignore the teasing and act as though it doesn't bother him, the teasers will pick on someone else. The more he reacts, the more the teasers will focus on him

Of course, you also want to reassure your son that being short is no fault—that in fact many great thinkers and doers in history have been short.

Most important is that you not become trapped in feelings that you are responsible for his unhappiness. The more you can convey your love for your son and your belief in how wonderful he is as he is, the less vulnerable he will be to other's negative remarks. After all, it's your opinion that matters most to him. If you admire him just as he is, he will feel good about himself. He will be both happier and also better able to weather the unpleasant experience of being teased.

How can I help my nine-year-old stop sucking her thumb?

Q My daughter discovered her thumb at two months old, and I was delighted that she had found a self-soothing activity. However, she's now nine years old, already a couple of years into orthodontia (head gear) and is not ready to quit. I do believe she has cut back or eliminated sucking at school, but still does it in some social situations.

Part of me believes that this is something (like potty training) that is simply in her control and not mine. But I wonder if I should worry, or if I can suggest other comforting actions to help take up the slack when she is ready to stop.

A You are right that there is nothing you can (or should) do to force your daughter to stop sucking her thumb, but there are ways to help her. First, however, you need to know what her motivation is. Does she actively want to stop but feel she can't? Or does she resent efforts to get her to give up her thumb?

If she wants help stopping, ask her what ideas she has about better ways of feeling soothed. Offer her alternatives that would be more age-appropriate and less harmful to her teeth, such as a supply of sugar-free candy or gum, carrot sticks or celery. Also, help her to identify situations in which her thumb-sucking feels irresistible, and suggest that she prepare for those times by thinking of other ways of comforting herself and by having something else available to suck or chew if necessary,

If your daughter does not see the necessity to stop sucking her thumb, consider what might be causing her to need this kind of comfort. You don't say how the rest of her life is going, but perhaps she is under too much pressure. Maybe she is overwhelmed with extracurricular activities or you are unintentionally expecting behavior from her that is more "grown-up" than she can easily achieve.

Once you have removed any unnecessary pressure and have brought all of your expectations of her in line with her age, you might then try to have dialogue with her about the thumb sucking. Suggest that perhaps she is looking to her thumb for comfort in response to aspects of her life that are upsetting her, ask what these might be, and let her know that you would like to try to help her reduce these sources of stress.

You may also consider arranging for her orthodontist to have a friendly discussion with your daughter about the effect her thumb-sucking is having on her teeth and on the length of time she will need braces. It is possible that the doctor's authority plus her desire to graduate from wearing braces may help her to stop.

Most important is to keep the big picture in mind: her thumb-sucking is decreasing gradually and will probably end before too much more time passes.

How can I help my daughter shed the excess pounds?

Q My husband and I read your column every month and really find it helpful. We are hoping you can help us with a problem in our own family.

Our nine-year-old daughter is quite overweight. I know this is unhealthy for her, and I want to help her shed the excess pounds. I have had her to the pediatrician, who says there is absolutely no physical reason for her to be overweight and that the problem is emotional.

I also have to admit that my husband and I are each carrying an extra thirty pounds or so, so I am sure this has something to do with our daughter's problem. We have both tried lots of diets without much success. Suggestions?

A Most likely, you are correct in thinking that a major cause of your daughter's struggles with her weight is her unconscious desire to look like her parents. On the bright side, perhaps your wish to help your daughter become healthier will motivate your husband and yourself to lose pounds as well.

We suggest that you make this a real family project. Choose and plan healthy meals, take family walks or bike rides for exercise, have a weekly weigh-in and, generally, show your daughter that you are all in this together. It will be much easier for your daughter to change her eating habits if she doesn't feel she is the only one who is being asked to make sacrifices.

Most important, everyone must realize that some backsliding is both inevitable and also a sign of progress. If you, your husband or your daughter temporarily go off the diet and exercise plan, that does not mean that the task is too difficult or that the backslider is unable to succeed. We define progress in a self-improvement program as "more success than failure over time."

If you use moments of backsliding as occasions to identify troublesome temptations, to support each other and to renew your determination, there is every reason to think your whole family can succeed in reaching a healthy weight.

What's the best way to help a child control her weight?

Q I love reading the Smart Love column in Chicago Parent magazine. I would like to ask this question and hope for the best.

My daughter is eight years old and is overweight (or as she puts it, "extra weight"). We don't eat junk food, sweets and dessert too often. She is aware of her extra weight and on a couple of occasions has been teased about it in school, which has bothered her. We have her involved in soccer, basketball and swimming, depending on the season, to try and keep her physically active.

When I discussed her weight with her pediatrician, his statement was basically the amount of food intake vs. physical activity. She seems to require a lot more food than other kids to be satisfied. Her appetite seems to be a lot bigger than kids her age. Sometimes, she will get angry at us when we tell her that she can't have seconds and that she has to eat more salad or vegetables.

We need help in trying to help her control her weight now before it becomes a lifetime struggle which, by the way, her Dad, my husband, has battled with all his life.

A First we suggest that you examine your own approach to your daughter and food. Without realizing it, many parents use food as a reward. They tell their children that if they clean their room or help out with a younger sibling, they can have a treat. When food takes on the meaning of parental love and a job well done, children are more likely to eat when they are not hungry.

You also want to be careful not to resort to punitive measures in the attempt to help your daughter develop better eating habits. Telling your daughter she can't have seconds or that she has to eat extra portions of foods she doesn't like will incline her to become a secret snacker. It is crucial to enlist your daughter's cooperation before you work on restricting her calories.

Second, since, like all children, your daughter wants to be just like her parents, there is another possible reason she is turning to food for comfort—she is emulating her Dad. In the absence of a metabolic defect (which your daughter doesn't appear to have, as she has been seen by her pediatrician), the main reason people gain weight is that they eat when they aren't hungry.

Since your husband apparently has this problem, we suggest that you enlist his help. He might sit down with your daughter and share his own struggles with eating and ask if she would like to work with him to develop healthier eating habits and a better weight. Father and daughter can make a diet plan together and meet every day in a mutually supportive manner to discuss successes or problems. They can have a daily or weekly weigh-in to check their progress. (Do ask your pediatrician to tell you what a healthy weight is for your daughter.)

You can help by keeping the cupboard free of snacks that are high in fats or calories and by finding and making creative recipes for healthy foods. With this kind of support and shared goals, your daughter will find it much easier to reach and maintain an appropriate weight and your husband will benefit as well.

Chapter Two
Teens

Bracing for a stormy adolescence

Q Ever since my nine-year-old daughter was a toddler, people who know her well have warned me, "You're in for a stormy adolescence." I understand why they think this. She's a high-energy and high-intensity kid, very sensitive and passionate. But I generally resist the idea of labeling kids and fear that making this assumption may be a self-fulfilling prophesy.

Now that adolescence is just around the corner, I'm wondering two things: does a child's temperament really affect how difficult she will be during her adolescent years, and is there really anything I can do now to pave the way for making that period as harmonious as possible?

A The fact that your daughter is "high-energy and high-intensity" in no way implies that her adolescence will be stormy. In fact, adolescents who are intense and energetic often are very accomplished and manage successfully to juggle school, recreational activities, and friendships.

Actually, the most important determinant of the kind of adolescence a child will have is the nature of her relationship with you. A stormy adolescence is an adolescence in which parents feel that they don't know what is happening with their child, the child is behaving in ways of which the parents don't approve, or the child adamantly resists parental input and oversight. All of this unhappiness can be avoided if parents manage to establish a close relationship with their child in the preteen years.

The key to becoming a parent to whom your child looks for

guidance and in whom your child wants to confide is to not expect the child to be more grown up than her age warrants, to manage her behavior with kindness rather than discipline, and always to show her that you love and care for her.

You don't say what your relationship with your daughter is like, but clearly you feel very positively about her. When children feel loved and appreciated by their parents, they are likely to confide in them and to trust them. If your daughter looks to you for help and comfort now, she will continue to do so when she encounters problems in adolescence.

The most important action you can take now to insure a harmonious adolescence is to spend lots of positive time with your daughter and to listen carefully and sympathetically to her ideas and point of view. It is a myth that adolescents need to rebel and distance themselves from parents during adolescence. What they truly need and want more than anything is to have parents they can confide in and consult. If you continue to create an atmosphere in which your daughter feels comfortable sharing her feelings and asking your advice, you will find that your daughter's adolescence will not be stormy and that it will only deepen your relationship.

Preteens who don't 'open up'

Q How should I react when my preteen daughter (she's eleven going on twenty-one) gets into a pouty mood and just mopes around, complaining that nothing is fair and stirring up arguments with her eight-year-old brother? I've tried reasoning with her, but that tends to make it worse. She just gets defensive and it's hard for me not to get emotional about it. She never wants to talk about what's bothering her. Sometimes I get the impression she really doesn't know what's bothering her, and it may be hormones more than anything else. What would you suggest I try? Thanks.

A It's possible that both you and she are reacting to her maturation. Without more information, it's hard to know, but perhaps on your side you are expecting too much of her now that she is older. Or maybe you have not taken her newfound maturity into account and are not giving her enough scope for choices and decisions.

Either way, it's usually the case that if you show children that you really are interested in their feelings, they will eventually open up to you. While we can understand your impulse to "reason" with your daughter when she feels badly, she may well experience you as arguing with her and as saying that her feelings aren't real or don't count. So, initially, it would be more helpful to offer a sympathetic ear without challenging her perceptions. The same approach will work if her discontent has less to do with you and more to do with increased school demands or problems with peers.

Another strategy for improving your relationship with your daughter is to try to find time to spend with her doing something she really enjoys. As you spend pleasant time together, her feelings of being uncared for will soften. Even an hour or two once a week can work wonders. It is all too easy to fall into the trap of relating to our children around tasks and duties and to overlook opportunities for happy, unpressured moments.

Early adolescent attitude

Q My ten-year-old daughter has developed an "attitude," and it seems to get worse when she spends a lot of time with her friends. At home, she's become surly, impatient, uncommunicative and abrasive—flouncing about like a put-upon teenager. With her friends, on the other hand, she's animated, exuberant and thoroughly charming. These are kids she's known since preschool. I'd expect this split personality-type behavior from a thirteen- or fourteen-year-old (and I'd probably tolerate it, chalking it up to adolescence). But I'm afraid that if I let her get away with it now, other precocious behaviors won't be far behind—and may be even harder to handle. How should I handle this?

A We have been hearing from many parents that emotions that characterize adolescence seem to be appearing earlier and earlier. You don't say whether your daughter has begun menstruating yet, but if she has or if she is going through the physical changes that precede menstruation, the surge in hormones could be affecting her moods as well.

Also, if you can find a time when your daughter seems willing to talk, try to find out if there is something upsetting her, especially problems with friends or schoolwork. Often children will show a brave and charming face to the rest of the world and let down their hair at home.

In general, if your daughter is cranky with you but is functioning well in the rest of her life, there is probably no need to worry. You have created a sufficiently nurturing environment that she feels safe blowing off steam at home, and that release frees her to be delightful with friends and others outside the family. If you understand that you are helping your daughter by allowing her some room to be moody and grouchy, it may make it easier to get through this period. There is no reason to fear that tolerating her dramatic moments will encourage her to engage in an unhealthy type of precocity. On the contrary, by cutting her some emotional slack, you make her feel understood and loved. She will feel inspired to treat herself with the same caring you show her, and will be less likely to engage in self-destructive behaviors.

Should I restrict how my child spends her allowance?

Q What is your approach to allowances? My eleven-year-old gets $10 a week of spending money.

We think she is spending too much of it on frivolous purchases such as rap music, candy and soft drinks, but when we try to talk to her about this, she says it's her money and she should be able to spend it how she wants. Also, she sometimes talks back, doesn't get her homework done and talks on the phone after she is supposed to be in bed.

We have told her we will dock her $1 for each of these infractions, but she gets upset, says we are horrible and unfair and sulks for days. We really need help thinking this through.

A We admire your willingness to reconsider your policies when they are making your child unhappy.

In this case, we have to agree with your daughter that her allowance is hers to spend as she wishes. She gets less than $1.50 a day, so if she wants something that costs more than $1.50, she will learn to save. Just as adults like to have a little money to spend just for fun, that outlet is good for children as well.

We do not advocate tying children's allowances to good behavior, including doing chores or homework. An allowance should not be a reward but a treat children can enjoy with no strings attached. When allowances are seen as rewards for behavior, children feel coerced into the behavior or resentful when the money is withheld. They do not learn to enjoy doing chores or schoolwork.

If children are not doing well in school, aren't going to bed on time or are resisting chores, those issues need to be dealt with independently. For example, nightly bed checks might completely solve the after-hours phone conversations.

Helping kids make better decisions

Q At what age should parents allow kids to make bad choices instead of arguing with them about things when we know they won't do what we say? Like wearing a bike helmet (my son is twelve)? Or not smoking? (My daughter is sixteen)?

A Actually, parenting is a lifetime commitment and opportunity in the sense that you will always be tremendously influential in your children's lives (their occasional denials notwithstanding). So it is crucial that you never "allow" your children to make choices that can harm them physically or emotionally.

If you permit your son not to wear a bike helmet, or your daughter to smoke, deep down they will conclude that you don't care whether they are safe and sound, or worse, that you want them to hurt themselves. On the other hand, if you take a strong stand and show your children that you will do everything you can do to keep them from harm you will strengthen their own wishes to care for themselves.

So if your son won't wear a bike helmet, take away his bike. If you find your daughter's cigarettes, throw them away and don't let her smoke in your house or in your presence. Trust us when we say that your opinion is much more important to your children than you imagine, and that if you take the unswerving position that you will do everything in your power to keep your children safe, over time they will want to be safe as well.

Help for handling bedtimes

Q My sixth grader wants to set her own bedtime on school nights. She's a responsible, conscientious student who manages her time well. Until now, her weeknight bedtime has been 9:30 p.m. Even then, it's sometimes hard to get her out of bed in the morning. I told her I'd agree to 10:00 p.m. if she'd agree to spent the extra half hour reading, not watching TV. But she doesn't want any limitation on how late she stays up or what she does. Can you help us settle this matter?

A When making rules for your child, it often helps to refocus on the reason for the rule. Children need set bedtimes because they are too immature to think about future consequences when there is pleasure in the present they want to pursue. So left to their own devices, they are likely to play into the wee hours and then feel tired and out of sorts when morning comes.

Since your daughter is having trouble getting up in the morning as it is, she probably should not have a later bedtime. Explain to her that her bedtime stays at 9:30 p.m. until she needs fewer hours of sleep and feels less tired in the morning.

At the same time, it is important to recognize that you can only give her the opportunity to sleep – you can't force her to go to sleep. So at bedtime she should be in her room pursuing quiet activities like reading or listening to music. TV is too stimulating for a bedtime activity and she should do her TV watching earlier in the day.

Your daughter's wish not to have any limitation on how late she stays up or what she does is typical of all children who believe they are infallible when it comes to making decisions about their own welfare. Just as you protected your daughter when as a toddler she wanted to touch the hot stove or climb on unstable objects, you need to safeguard her welfare now and insist that she follow bedtime rules that will ensure that she gets enough sleep. If you enforce your rules gently but firmly and remain friendly in the process, she may grumble, but she will know your decision is based on caring and concern. She will not only get a good night's rest, but she will follow your example and her ability to make positive, caring decisions for herself will be strengthened.

Should I say no to my daughter's piercing?

Q What is your view about body piercing? My teen wants to get her nose pierced. I find the idea totally repulsive, but she insists that lots of her friends have done this and she thinks it looks "cool."

At first, I just said "no," but she has been begging and begging. I told her that I was worried she would pick up a disease from an unsterilized needle, but she says the place her friends go for piercing guarantees the procedure is sterile and that I can check that out if I want.

It goes against the grain to just say "no" in an arbitrary way, but I don't have any other real arguments except that I just don't like the idea. She says I am just out of touch and old fashioned. What's your advice?

A If body piercing is not against your religious beliefs, and if you find that it can be done safely, consider allowing your daughter to go ahead.

Just as you probably let her wear clothes that are not exactly to your taste as long as they are appropriate for her age, the fact that you find nose piercing unattractive is probably not a sufficient reason to forbid her from doing it. Moreover, unlike tattoos, which are extremely difficult to remove, piercings will grow together and disappear if the wearer stops wearing the jewelry that is keeping them open. So your daughter always has the option of changing her mind if she decides she no longer likes the look.

Do better clothes make better friends?

Q My daughter has just started sixth grade and for the first time is finding it difficult to make and keep friends. She says there is no one she is interested in having for a friend. She says all the girls think about is boys and clothes and she thinks that is stupid. My daughter is a bit of a tomboy and her idea of what to wear to school is an old pair of jeans and a sweatshirt. Should I try to get her to dress more attractively in hopes that she will fit in better? I hate to see her unhappy, but I don't know how to help her.

A This is commonly a difficult age for girls; the problems your daughter is having are not unusual. There is a wide variation in the rate at which girls make the transition to being full-fledged teens. Your daughter is well within the norm for girls her age. Moreover, you can consider yourself lucky. It is much more difficult to be the parent of a daughter who is growing up very fast than to be the parent of a daughter, like yours, who is taking her time.

The gift you can give your daughter is not to pressure her. Rather, you should reassure her she is fine and applaud her. Tell her that you admire her unwillingness to pretend to be more sophisticated just to have more friends. You might suggest that she consider whether there are other girls in her grade who are more like her. She doesn't need a million friends; one or two good ones will help a lot. You may not realize it, but your opinion is still the one that means the most to your daughter.

Careless about appearance

Q My ten-year-old daughter seems entirely unconcerned about her grooming and clothing. She tells me "That kind of thing really doesn't matter, Dad." Now she is getting to the age where I think it may start to matter socially. She is among the less socially mature of her friends and classmates. I don't want to wait until she is picked on or ostracized because that kind of thing can stick for a long time even after you clean up your act. But I also don't want to be picking on her myself. What are your thoughts on this?

A At a time when most parents are worried because their children seem to be growing up too fast and trying to look eighteen when they are only ten, you are fortunate that your daughter is content to look and act her age. Try to avoid sending her the message that you want her to appear more sophisticated. Instead, you can feel proud that you have succeeded in raising a daughter who is comfortable listening to her inner clock and who is not swayed by peer pressure to look older than she feels. Because your opinion carries a lot of weight with your daughter, you will be of most help to her if you make clear that you are in no hurry to have her look grown-up and that you think it is wonderful that she is following her own timetable.

We do not think you need to worry about your daughter being picked on or ostracized. She sounds as though she has both feet firmly planted on the ground, and we bet she will not choose friends who judge others solely on appearance.

Our unhappy preteen seems depressed and friendless

Q My twelve-year-old daughter has been very unhappy at school all fall. She complains that no one likes her. She says her friends from last year are snubbing her and other kids do not seem interested.

I have noticed she is withdrawn and that when we talk to her she tends to answer in monosyllables. She also complains a lot about stomachaches and headaches during the week but we notice that she doesn't seem to feel sick on the weekends. We don't know how to help her. Until now she has been a pretty happy kid, but at this point she doesn't seem to be enjoying life.

A This is a hard question to answer because it is not clear whether your daughter's depression is the cause or whether she is depressed in response to the events at school. The best strategy is to approach the problem from both angles. You also need to investigate the possibility of an underlying physical problem.

First, your daughter's pediatrician should examine her to ensure her physical complaints are not symptoms of a more serious problem. If she is all right, then try concrete help in making friends. Think of some activities such as going to a movie, bowling or bike riding, and suggest she invite a friend or two along. That may help start a friendship and you will have a chance to observe her with her friends. Notice whether she is unknowingly coming across as aloof, sarcastic or unfriendly. If you see she is getting in her own way, try to explain this to her as gently and diplomatically as possible. Then give her some strategies for approaching peers, such as asking them about their interests and avoiding monosyllabic answers.

In trying to understand why your daughter might be withdrawing and feeling depressed, you might also consider whether there have been recent dislocations in the family, such as illness, divorce, work-related problems or financial problems that might be affecting her. Ask her if she has things on her mind that are bothering or worrying her. Investigate whether she is upset about premenstrual changes in her body or the impending onset of menstruation. Most important, make clear to her that you know she is struggling right now and that you want to do everything in your power to help and you are available to talk.

Time-outs and other disciplines are power tools

Q I understand that spanking children is bad because it teaches them it is OK to inflict physical pain on others. But I really don't understand why you say that other disciplinary responses when children do something wrong, such as time-outs or taking away privileges like talking on the phone, are not OK. These responses do seem to work and I can't see how they are harming my children. Could you please explain your position?

A Don't forget discipline works only because we are bigger and stronger and because we control the resources they need. Given that the ultimate basis for our ability to manage our children's behavior is power, and given all children copy the way their parents treat them, how we use the power we have will shape the way our children treat themselves and how they treat others. Time-outs and consequences are emotionally harsh even though they are not physically violent. When children copy these strategies for handling differences of opinion, they may become adults who withdraw from relationships when the other disagrees with them or who use money or other material goods in controlling, punitive ways. This is why we advocate loving regulation as a way of managing children's behavior. In loving regulation, the parent steps in and regulates the behavior without ever adding unpleasant consequences such as time-outs. Loving regulation is nonviolent parenting; in this increasingly violent world, we need to raise our children to be adults who can tolerate others' differences without resorting to violence—physical or emotional.

Controlling a sweet tooth

Q I would like to get the Piepers' advice on an issue relating to children's eating habits. My ten-year-old daughter is slightly chubby. Not fat, but heavier than normal. She has a real sweet tooth and is always asking for dessert and shows no ability to resist anything that's sweet. I worry that she will get more overweight and this will become an issue she will struggle with for the rest of her life (I struggle to keep my weight down). But I don't want to encourage an eating disorder.

We try to keep mainly healthy foods in the house, but her older brother is a skinny guy who needs all the calories he can get, so we can't make sure everything in the house is okay to eat in whatever quantities she likes. Also, she does gymnastics and plays baseball, rides her bike and generally is pretty active.

A If your daughter is physically active and only slightly overweight, you may be more worried than is necessary. We would suggest a visit to your pediatrician, who can check your daughter's cholesterol, blood pressure, etc. You might suggest to your pediatrician ahead of time that if she finds your daughter to be overweight or if her blood tests are not normal, he speak with your daughter about the long-term importance of eating healthy foods and maintaining the proper weight for her frame.

Your pediatrician also may have some age-appropriate literature on nutrition that she can give your daughter. Your daughter will probably respond more constructively to this message if it comes from a neutral, authoritative source.

On the other hand, if your pediatrician finds that your daughter's weight and blood chemistry are normal, we suggest that you cease to focus on your daughter's eating and weight. You observe that regulating your eating is a struggle for you, but you don't necessarily want to conclude that it will be a problem for your daughter as well.

That said, it can't hurt to encourage your daughter's enjoyment of exercise. You might plan some regular family hikes or bike rides on weekends.

If I'm not there, how can I be sure he eats healthy?

Q My son, who is in sixth grade, is able to go to the cafeteria for the first time (previously he had to bring lunch). I have signed up and paid for him to be on the lunch plan for the entire year. I am concerned that he is mainly eating candy for lunch. I find tons of candy wrappers in his back pack and his answers about what he ate for lunch are vague. He is a little overweight, but mainly I am concerned about his teeth and his health. How can I get him to eat a healthy lunch?

A This is a common problem. At whatever age children gain control over their eating, they frequently do not make the wisest choices.

We suggest a dual approach. First, sit down with your son and explain why eating so much sugar is bad for him. Tell him you know he cares about his body and staying healthy, and emphasize that there is no reason he couldn't have one candy bar a day as long as the rest of the day he makes good food choices.

Get him an age-appropriate book about nutrition. You might make an appointment with his doctor to talk to him about the importance of good eating habits. At the same time, approach the school. Investigate whether the lunch plan can be modified to limit the amount of sweets a child can get at any one meal. Often biology teachers are happy to spend class time explaining why growing children need to include a variety of food groups in their diets.

Finally, think about what is being communicated to your son about sweets by the family culture. If you eat a lot of sweets, he may be copying you. In that case, maybe the whole family could go on a "sweets diet." On the other hand, if candy is never allowed, children can react by seeking it out at school and friends' houses. This is why it is important to make clear to your son that sweets are fine in moderation.

Don't ignore a child's gun fascination

Q My son came home from sixth grade today telling me a boy in his class has started to make a gun with his fist and pretend to shoot other kids. The boy also told some kids that he knows where his father keeps his hunting rifles—and knows how to shoot them. Then he added, "I'm just kidding—I don't want to be in the headlines." This boy is unpopular and has few friends. My son says he is afraid of this boy and is worried about going to school. I told him I am sure he will be OK if he stays away from the boy and doesn't provoke him. But I wonder if I should do something more.

A You need to take preventive measures. Before almost every school shooting there are warning signs—such as those you describe—that are ignored. It is better to take measures that may prove unnecessary than not act and have a tragedy occur. Contact the school administration with your concerns and ask what they intend to do. If the school is unwilling to have the boy evaluated psychologically and take steps to ensure he doesn't bring weapons to school, you can call the police. Children who talk about shooting other children must be taken seriously and considered a threat to the entire community as well as to themselves.

Does it help or hurt my teen when I bail him out?

Q My teenager is basically a good student, but he is also somewhat disorganized and forgetful. On a number of occasions, he has left his homework at home.

He always wants me to write a note to his teacher saying that he did the work but left it at home, which is true. Apparently, he still gets marked off a little because the work is late, but not as much as if I didn't write the note saying that he did the homework. Friends say I am enabling his disorganization by writing these notes and that I should tell him I will no longer bail him out when he forgets his assignments. What do you think?

A You are not "enabling" your son's behavior, because it is normal – all adolescents are disorganized and forgetful at times.

Keep in mind that even though your son may have the body of a man, he still needs your help. For example, ask him before he heads off for school if he has done his homework and even check his room. If he does forget his homework, do help him out by writing a note. You are the model for his relation to himself and others, and it is much better to model compassion and helpfulness than punitiveness and negativity.

Letting him suffer when you could be a part of the solution doesn't teach him anything valuable. In fact, it gives him the message that he doesn't deserve help when he errs.

How do I keep my teen from instant messaging?

Q How do you control your teenager's time when she is supposed to be doing homework and I think she is mainly instant messaging her friends? Whenever I walk into my sixteen-year-old daughter's room, she is at her computer and she hides what is on the screen. Once in a while she isn't fast enough, and I see the IM screen. She is actually doing OK in school, but I think this is causing her to stay up later than she would have to if she just did her homework and I am not sure she is getting enough sleep. I have made rules about no instant messaging until after her homework is done, but I have no way to enforce it because she does her homework at her computer and I can't really watch her screen every minute. We can't keep her off the Internet because we have wireless all over the house. Suggestions?

A The rule of thumb with teenagers is not to get into unnecessary conflicts with them and to save your authority over them for when you really need it. Your daughter's behavior is in keeping with the relatively new phenomenon that many teens prefer instant messaging on computers, and text messaging on cell phones, to actual phone conversations with their friends. Nonetheless, as long as your daughter is doing well in school, count your blessings and don't confront her over the instant messaging. Perhaps it is robbing her of a little sleep, but if she is sufficiently tired she will want to get rest. She will be more likely to get a good night's sleep on her own if her bedtime has not become an issue between you. Otherwise, there seems little harm in what she is doing. Make clear to your daughter that as long as her grades remain good, she can make her own choices about the rhythm of her evenings. Then you can save your interventions for really important health and safety issues, such as getting in by curfew, letting you know where she will be when she goes out with friends, and so on.

Punishment won't stop homework war

Q My fifth grader's science teacher called to say my son has not been handing in his homework. The teacher said he has talked to my son and my son apologizes, offers an excuse and promises to bring it the next day, but doesn't.

Meanwhile, my son's grades are slipping because he hasn't mastered the material covered in the homework. The teacher wants us to get involved. I think we should ground him from his traveling basketball team, but my husband thinks that would be too tough on him. He wants to take away his allowance for a week or two. I want to make enough of an impression on my son that he won't do this again. What do you advise?

A To solve this problem, you must first find out why your son is not doing his homework. The most likely explanation is that he didn't understand some of the early material, so he is having more trouble now. If this is the case, sit down with him in a positive frame of mind and review all the material back to the point he stopped doing homework. Once he understands the concepts and is ready to start doing the missing homework, make yourself available to help.

Your son has somehow gotten the idea that he can't turn to you when things go wrong in school. To avoid another episode like this in the future, you need to let him know everyone has difficulty with homework sometimes and you are always happy to help.

It's also possible your son needs help organizing his time. Again, this indicates he needs help, not punishment. When he gets home from school go over what is due the next day and ask his input on making a schedule for getting everything finished. If you have quiet work to do, suggest that he might like to sit with you and do his assignments. In short, your son needs your help, not disapproval and punishments. If you assist him now, he should be able to get back on track at school.

Hostility to schoolwork

Q According to his teacher, my fifth grader is not working to his potential. We know that he puts off doing his homework and then rushes through it. We have tried holding back his allowance and restricting him from activities, but that didn't work. In fact he became very sulky. My friends suggest offering him rewards like renting a video he likes. What do you think would help?

A First we suggest that neither punishments nor rewards will solve the real problem, which is that for some reason your son is not enjoying the learning experience. Punishing him only made him dislike his studies more. If you entice him with rewards, he may work for the reward, but that will not introduce him to the pleasure of learning. When the rewards cease, his motivation will run out of steam.

The best long-term solution is to find a way to help your son enjoy his studies. The first step is to show him that you are on his side. Ask him how he feels about school—which subjects he likes, and which subjects are causing him trouble. Then ask what you can do to help. Perhaps he would like to have a tutor who would help him with the subjects with which he is struggling.

One strategy we have found effective is to invite him to be in the same room with you when he is doing his homework, so that he will have an adult available to answer questions as they arise. Because your goal is to show him that learning can be fun, do your very best to be positive and never negative when answering his questions. For example, if he has made a mistake, rather than telling him he has done something wrong, tell him he made a good try. Rather than just giving him the answer, show him how to divide the question into small steps that will lead to an answer.

The best way to discover that learning can be fun is to share the problem-solving effort with someone who is positive and enthusiastic. If you can be that person for your son, or you can find a tutor who offers these qualities, your son's natural curiosity will be stimulated and he will begin to get more enjoyment from his studies.

How do I deal with my son and his homework lies?

Q What do you do when your child doesn't tell you the truth about handing in homework?

I check with my thirteen-year-old son every day about whether his homework is done and he always says it is. I just went for a parent-teacher conference, and his advisor told me that he is inconsistent about getting homework done in each of his courses. And, of course, when he doesn't do his homework, he can't do well on tests and quizzes. As a result, he is doing quite badly.

I have talked and talked to him about the importance of doing well in school to his future life, but I am obviously not getting through. I am thinking about grounding him or taking away his TV privileges until I get a good report.

A Actually, this is a fairly common problem. Like younger children, teenagers often bend the truth to avoid unpleasantness.

The solution is not to punish your son, which will only make him feel alienated and more inclined to hide bad news from you, but to show him that you will help him and work with him.

Let him know that you realize that at this moment in his life he needs help getting his work done. Tell him that you are going to contact each of his teachers and request that they e-mail or fax you his homework schedule and contact you immediately if an assignment is not handed in. Teachers are usually willing to do this for parents of struggling children.

Offer daily to help your son with assignments he finds difficult. Insist that he do his homework first before he watches TV or talks with his friends on the phone. Go over the homework with him to make sure that it is done well and that he understands the assignment. Most important, remain friendly and positive so that your son sees you as being on his side.

Over time, the good habits you instill will become second nature to him and he will be increasingly able to assume responsibility for getting his work done well and on time.

How can I trust my thirteen-year-old after he lied to me?

Q My thirteen-year-old son told me he was going to stay after school and see a teacher for help with math. When he got home, I asked him how it had gone and he said the teacher had been helpful. That night I heard him on the phone with one of his friends talking about something that had happened when they were hanging out at a video game parlor in the mall that afternoon. I was so shocked and angry that he had lied to me that I grounded him for a month, and I have to admit I also yelled quite a bit. Now I feel I hardly know my son and I certainly don't trust him. How do I prevent him from doing this again?

A We can understand your shock and dismay at discovering that your son had been so very deceptive. But the problem lies less with your son and more with the relationship that has evolved between you. You need to sit down with him and tell him that something has obviously gone wrong in your relationship because he doesn't feel he can tell you what plans he would like to make and trust that if you say "No," it will be for a good reason. Emphasize that you are not looking for opportunities to frustrate him. On the contrary, you want whenever possible to endorse his choices. For example, if the mall is safe and he has been getting his school work done, you might as well let him play video games with a friend for an hour after school—but only if he asks you. Explain that for his own good and your peace of mind, it is never acceptable for him to go places without telling you and that if he continues to do so, you will have to make sure you or someone else picks him up after school. This is a way of making sure your son is safe without punishing him. If your son responds to you by making his wish to spend time with his friends known, do reinforce his openness by listening carefully and facilitating his choices whenever possible.

Do I punish my teen who never lied to me before?

Q My son is a freshman in high school. Until now he has been very responsible and so we have given him a lot of leeway. When he says he is going to a friend's house, we have not really checked up on him. Last week, however, he told us that he was going to a friend's house and when I called there to see if he wanted a ride home, the friend's mother said he and the friend were at "teen night" at one of the disco clubs in our area. I would probably have let him go if he had asked me, but I don't like the fact that he lied to me. I am inclined to ground him for two weeks, but I know you don't recommend this. What do you recommend?

A Because this is the first time your son has not been candid with you, there is no reason to pull out the big guns. On the other hand, you want to make clear that this kind of deception is not acceptable. Explain in a friendly but firm way that while he is old enough to go places on his own, the condition for this freedom is that he maintains good lines of communication with you and that you can trust him to be truthful.

Tell him that even though he feels quite grown up, you are responsible for his safety and you take that responsibility seriously. If he shows you he is trustworthy, you are willing to take his word for where he is and will give him as much leeway as possible to make plans with friends. On the other hand, if you find he isn't telling you the truth, you will be calling to check up on him and he will not be allowed to make plans that cannot be verified.

Once your position is clear to him, give him another chance to show you that he recognizes your legitimate concerns for his welfare and can be relied on to be honest with you about where he is and with whom.

Discussing menstruation with girls

Q I have two friends with nine-year-old daughters, neither of whom will discuss menstruation with their mothers. They want to get this information to the girls in a timely manner, but of course don't want to force it on them. Any ideas on how to open this subject in a non-threatening way? (In both cases, there are hereditary reasons to be prepared for early onset, say ten years old.)

A One of the best ways to introduce the topic of menstruation to girls who feel squeamish about discussing it is to give them one of the excellent books on the topic. Once they have read about the subject in privacy and have had a chance to think about it, girls will often feel more comfortable asking their mothers questions. One ten-year-old we know especially recommends *The Care and Keeping of You* by Valerie Lee Schaefer (Pleasant Company Publications, 1998) and *The Period Book* by Karen Gravelle (Walker & Co., 1996).

It may also help if the mothers share with their daughters their own experiences, including embarrassed feelings they may have had and their own difficulty discussing the subject with their mothers. If the mothers recount their own histories, including the age at which they began to menstruate, where they were when they got their first period, what it felt like, etc., odds are their daughters will be all ears!

Most important is that the mothers not mistake their daughters' discomfort at talking with them about menstruation for lack of interest in the topic. Nearly every girl is consumed with curiosity about the changes that are going to occur to her body, even though she may feel strongly that she cannot talk about these changes with her mother. Unfortunately, when they turn to their peers for advice, girls usually get as much misinformation as information. This is another good reason to give preteens books like the ones mentioned above.

Telling kids about your youthful indiscretions

Q I'm writing for advice on how to respond to children when they ask personal questions, especially when we as parents don't want to be dishonest or admit to past wrongdoing. My thirteen-year-old daughter has begun asking me about whether I tried cigarettes when I was a teenager. It won't be long before she asks me questions about whether I had sex before marriage or tried drugs. I grew up in the 70s and did a lot of things I wish I hadn't done and I hope she doesn't do. But how do I reply to these blunt questions?

A This is a tough problem and one that every parent struggles with. On the one hand, parents are tempted to describe in detail the youthful mistakes they made, both because they want to be honest with their children and also because they don't want to misrepresent themselves as perfect beings, which will make their children feel hopelessly imperfect. On the other hand, parents realize that because their children love and idealize them, they may respond to the details of parents' youthful errors by imitating behaviors their parents no longer view as good choices.

The best course is to compromise. Don't get into the specifics of what you regret having done. If you are too specific, your child may conclude that since you are her idol, it is OK for her to make the same errors. Rather, emphasize to your daughter that when you were her age or a little older, you tried things that were either bad for you or that required more maturity than you really possessed (for example, you had sex before you were emotionally ready to handle the consequences), and that you were sorry afterward. Use this opportunity to emphasize that you now know that it would have been much better if you had listened to the advice of the adults who cared about you. Tell your daughter that in retrospect, you can see that your parents and teachers were not trying to squelch your fun when they tried to set limits, but rather wanted to help you make good decisions for yourself. Explain that your only wish is to spare her from experiencing the pain of the kind of mistakes you made at her age.

Reticent teenager

Q My fourteen-year-old daughter has always been somewhat reticent. It's just part of her temperament. But it's gotten worse as she's gotten older. She feels that my asking, "Hi, How was your day?" is an invasion of privacy. She's at an age when I need to be able to talk to her about feelings, school, sex and drugs, but when I try to push her beyond monosyllabic answers, she gets angry and withdraws. Do you have any advice for getting past this? (She is my oldest child.)

A Actually, we would suggest that your daughter's reticence is not a permanent part of her personality, but rather results from what has clearly been a longstanding difficulty in communication between the two of you. Because the problem is not of recent origin, it will be harder to solve. Pressuring your daughter to communicate will simply cause her to withdraw further.

If there is something you need to tell your daughter about "feelings, school, sex, and drugs," explain that what you are about to tell her is important and ask her to listen, but don't lean on her to enter into a dialogue with you. Most important is to establish a relationship with your daughter in which she actively seeks you out as a confidant.

We suggest that you begin by showing her that contrary to her expectations, talking with you can be enjoyable. Initiate a conversation with her about something that interests her. Ask her specific questions about this topic, but be sure not to criticize or second-guess her when she is sharing her enthusiasm. As your daughter discovers that talking with you and basking in your warmth and admiration can be supremely enjoyable, she will want more of this pleasure. We are certain that you will be pleasantly surprised to discover that your daughter has a multitude of pent-up wishes to confide in you.

Unapproachable teenage daughter

Q My seventeen-year-old daughter doesn't like me talking to her. She is either watching TV shows or talking on the phone with her friends when I come home from work. The words she uses are "be quiet" or "shut up," even if I only say "hi." It has gotten to the point where I feel almost unwelcome in my own house.

I have asked her to be more respectful and realize a mom needs conversation. She is doing better. When I said "shut up" when I was young, my mom chased after me with a bar of soap to wash my mouth out. Today kids just run away or try and hit you if you try that. What should I do? It's an everyday thing to cope with.

A Your frustration at your inability to get through to your daughter is understandable because you are encountering a level of hostility that is not part of a normal developmental process. We suggest that you go all out for a month or two to improve the relationship, but if your daughter continues to feel this alienated from you, you should consider seeking professional counseling to help both of you to renew and reestablish your relationship.

The best way to work at improving the relationship on your own is to fit your overtures to her rhythm. For example, when you get home from work, wait to start a conversation with your daughter until she is less preoccupied (during a commercial break, or between phone calls). Open the conversation with a positive comment, such as, "It's good to see you. How was your day?" Ask if she would like you to fix her something to eat. As your daughter seems to assume that interactions with you will be unpleasant, do your best to avoid all negative comments, including remarking on her unwillingness to be communicative.

If, in spite of your overtures, your daughter tells you to shut up or leave her alone, take this opportunity to tell her that you know that she has been feeling alienated from you and that you want to do everything you can to show her that you are "there" for her. Even though it is true that "moms need conversation," you will increase your chances of making a positive connection with your daughter if you resist your understandable wish to pressure her to talk.

If, after a month or two, you find that your efforts are not causing a marked improvement in your relationship with your daughter, do seek professional help. You are both missing out on the closeness that every mother and daughter deserve and need, and a knowledgeable professional can help you to reestablish that warmth.

Preteens who resist body changes

Q I have a ten-year-old daughter soon to be eleven. She has started developing breasts and so I talked with her about wearing a bra. Whenever I try to discuss anything like this with her she turns her head and ignores me. She won't talk about anything to do with her body changing, etc.

My twenty-one-year-old stepdaughter had bought her a book about all the changes a girl goes through. I know she has been reading it and I have even talked to her about it even though they are always one-sided conversations (me).

I asked her if she wanted to go pick out some bras, but she did not want to. I went to the store and bought several different styles and had her try them on. After an hour in the bathroom she came out and picked one. I told her she needed to wear it to school. The problem is I cannot get her to wear it at all. I told her that if she doesn't wear it to school she will be grounded. It is the second week of school and she still has not worn it.

Am I doing the right thing by grounding her? I don't want to get a call from the school saying that she needs to be wearing one. Her breasts are not big, but you can see them protruding. How do I get her to wear a bra and even discuss puberty with her? I am worried about what will happen when she gets her period.

A Your daughter is having a common reaction to puberty: she is upset by the changes in her body and rather than accept them, she wants to pretend they aren't happening.

Rather than trying to force her to face "reality," you need to show her that you understand what she is going through. Talk with her about the fact that while all little girls' bodies change into women's bodies, this transformation sometimes occurs before the girl feels ready, and that can be very difficult because there is no holding back nature.

Certainly there is no reason to ground your daughter for having these feelings. We suggest that you be as diplomatic as possible and not force the issue so as to give your daughter some time to get used to the idea that she is developing a woman's body. If she can't tolerate the idea of wearing a bra, tell her that she has a choice: she can wear loose-fitting tops without a bra, or more fitted tops with a bra. Because the changes in her body are occurring against her wishes, giving her a sense of control wherever possible will ease the transition.

If you sympathize with your daughter's feelings, are diplomatic and give your daughter a little time to get used to the changes that are taking place, she will accept the inevitable. She will then be ready to talk with you about the next big event—menstruation.

Setting limits on tweens

Q My ten-year-old, fifth grade daughter has always been a little ahead of the curve on being fashionable and hip. She's always asking for permission to do things that I didn't think I'd have to discuss until she was closer to thirteen: getting her ears double pierced, wearing make-up, going to boy/girl dances, wearing platform shoes, and asking for the freedom to go places that "all her friends" are allowed to go (many of them are eleven years old) without adult supervision, such as shopping.

She's generally a pretty well-behaved kid, though her judgment is just what you'd expect of a child her age. My question is, how do I know if she's too young? How much do I have to have solid reasons and explain them to her when I simply feel she's too young for these things? And how do I support my "no's" when some of her friends' mothers are saying "yes?"

A You should say "no" to requests when saying "yes" makes you uneasy. You know your daughter and the environment in which she navigates. Just as you decided how near to the street it was safe for her to play at age two, or whether she could sled down the big hill or needed to stay on the small one when she was six, you are the best person to decide questions such as whether she should wear make-up or whether she can go to boy/girl dances.

Just as it was when she was younger, the most important criterion is preserving your daughter's health and safety. It is not safe for her to leave the house looking years older than her age, to be left for hours in unchaperoned settings with boys, or to shop for long periods with no adult supervision.

If you know you will be worried if you agree to a request, this is a sign that you shouldn't grant it. Support your decision by telling your daughter that you are doing your best to keep her safe and sound, and that it doesn't really matter whether other parents make different choices – you are making the choice you believe to be in her best interest.

We recommend that at times when you must say "no," you make every effort to help your daughter have as much of what she wants as possible. For example, if you don't want her wearing make-up and platform heels on the street, she certainly can wear them at home. Or if you don't think she should shop by herself with friends, you can offer to go along and get a cup of coffee while the girls look around. By accommodating your daughter's wishes whenever possible, you show her that you are not trying to spoil her fun, but rather that you want her to have fun that is safe and healthy. She will have this wonderful model to follow in years to come, when she is on her own and making important decisions for herself.

How do I handle a homesick camper?

Q What should I do when my 10-year-old gets homesick and wants to come home from overnight camp? He said he wanted to go, he has friends there and it's only four weeks. But after one week, he is demanding to come home. He says he doesn't like his counselor, he can't stand the food and some of the kids are picking on him.

He have paid the money and can't get it back. I'm certainly not going to pay for day camp at home on top of the money we have paid for camp, so my son would have to hang around the house and I'm sure he would be totally bored in about a day. He is really insisting, though, and says that if we love him, we will come get him. We really have no idea how to handle this.

A First, we suggest you focus on helping your son stay. Talk to the camp director and mention the problem between your son and the counselor and the fact that he is being picked on. Perhaps changing cabins would do the trick. Also, if it's allowed, send some familiar, favorite foods from home.

When you talk to your son, emphasize that if he comes home you won't be able to provide the kind of enjoyable activities available at camp and you are worried he will become bored and restless. Then, ask if he wouldn't be willing to give the camp at least one more week.

If your son remains convinced that camp is intolerable, let him come home. Unlike school, camp is optional and recreational. The money is spent whether he stays, and there is nothing to gain and much to lose by forcing him to remain. If you refuse to let him come home, he may feel you are indifferent to his feelings and become less likely to talk to you about issues he needs help with. He may also become less willing to try new things on the assumption that he will have no escape route if they don't work out.

By letting him come home, though, you show him that you are responsive to his suffering and make it more likely that he will try an overnight adventure or other new endeavors at a later date.

Our Teen Is Not Being Honest

Q Our teenage daughter has been lying to us about where she is after school. We have forbidden her to go on single dates with boys and she says she doesn't. But when she says she is gong to a friend's house and we call the friend's house, she isn't there. We think she might have a boyfriend, and we feel very strongly that she shouldn't be alone with boys at her age. We are tempted to ground her, but she is a good student and never gives us any other trouble. Suggestions?

A You need to open better lines of communication with your daughter. Sit down with her and tell her that you realize she doesn't feel she can tell you what she is doing after school. Emphasize that you just want to keep her out of situations that might be bad for her. Say that you really want to know why she doesn't feel she can be open with you. Listen carefully to her point of view. For example, she might admit that she is interested in a boy and that she doesn't see why she can't go to a movie without a chaperone. You might agree to relax your rules and allow her to be with a boy in public places if she agrees to be honest about her activities.

It is often helpful to ask your teen what rules would make sense to her. She may come up with guidelines you can endorse, such as agreeing not to be alone with a boy in a closed room. If you show your daughter that you are reasonable rather than autocratic, she will be much more likely to be open. In contrast, grounding her would just make her more alienated and resentful.

How to teach kids virtue

Q I have three boys, ages ten, six and four. My six- and four-year-olds play wonderfully together, always compromising and working out their disagreements. When my ten-year-old gets involved, the "fireworks" start. He and his six-year-old brother have very opposite personalities. My ten-year-old seems to always want to tease and leave out the six-year-old. He basically only wants to play with his youngest brother because they get along so well. I'm not sure how to handle this situation. Do I force him to play with both of them? Do I explain to him how incredibly unkind it is to leave his brother out, making him cry (believe me, I've tried). I'm at my wit's end, what should I do?

A You raise a problem that every parent confronts at some point, namely, how to teach virtue. As you have realized, lectures and shaming make children feel terrible, but don't change their behavior (at least when adults are not around). Forcing your ten-year-old to include the six-year-old in his play will prove just as counterproductive because it will make him angrier at the six-year-old and less inclined to play with him.

We are all born with a strong desire to become like those who are important to us. So the best way to teach children to share and to care is to treat them with compassion and generosity. Over time, children will emulate these positive responses and learn to be caring toward themselves and others.

When your ten-year-old is teasing your six-year-old, try to put your anger to one side and to offer a positive response your children can emulate. For example, you might ask the ten-year-old if he would like to play a game with you. The two younger children can then play peacefully and you have defused the situation without shaming or angering the ten-year-old. A second alternative is to let the ten-year-old and four-year-old play, and involve the six-year-old in a game or other activity. If, as is likely, the other two children ask to play with you and the remaining brother, you can include them, with the result that the ten-year-old will see both that you want to include everyone and also that it really is possible for all of the brothers to play together happily.

Helping children cope with tragedy

In the wake of the tragic events of September 11th, parents have repeatedly asked us how best to help their children cope when they are exposed to a horrifying reality. We would like to devote this column to a discussion of how to respond to your children so as to minimize the possibility that they will be traumatized by what they have heard or seen of the terrible events that have rocked the country.

For children under age fourteen, try to minimize their exposure to radio and television coverage of the disaster. You would not want your children to watch violent movies, and realistic descriptions of planes crashing into buildings and bodies falling out of the sky are more frightening than any movie.

Television images will be especially difficult for children to get out of their minds. Very young children may be especially frightened because their immaturity may cause them to believe that the scenes pictured are right in their neighborhood and are still happening.

Do not overwhelm children with information. When giving children bad news, it is always best to give the bare facts followed by reassurance that the worst is over. Then follow their lead about how much more they are ready to hear. When a young child who has heard that something bad has happened asks you what is wrong, you might say something like, "Some planes hit buildings and the buildings caught on fire." You might tell an older child, "Some very bad people stole airplanes and crashed them into buildings."

Ask children if they have any questions, but if they are not ready to talk, let them come to grips with the news on their own timetable.

One nine-year-old we know reacted to the grim news by trying to solve the problem. He responded cheerfully, "They should just cover the buildings with steel so airplanes wouldn't go through." He wasn't interested in further discussion and his parents didn't pressure him.

That night when they were putting their son to bed, his parents asked, "How are you feeling?" He burst into tears and said, "I want to move from our apartment to a small house that airplanes can't get to." At that point, he was ready to ask many questions about why people would behave that way and what had happened to the people in the buildings. He was also relieved to be reassured that there were no more airplanes with bad people in the sky.

Let your children know you are affected by the tragedy, while at the same time you show them you are optimistic about the future. Children often feel there is something wrong with being upset or expressing upset feelings; this is an opportunity to tell them that you and other adults feel troubled, too, because these events are really disturbing.

At the same time, it is important not to share with children pessimistic thoughts such as, "The world will never be the same," but to offer them optimism. "This is over now, and our government will catch the bad people who did this." Your children have such faith in your opinion, they will take your pessimism to mean that the whole world has become a terrible place, but they will also be very reassured by your optimism that things can get back to normal.

Try not to use tragedy as an object lesson about the world. This is not the moment to tell children, "See, there are bad people in the world; this is why you shouldn't talk to strangers." Children need to be reassured that they and the people they love are safe, and not to have their fears heightened.

Don't interfere with your children's coping mechanisms. Children have many ways of protecting themselves from the full awfulness of the tragedy. For example, they may make light of what has happened. One mother was horrified when her young child saw a photo of a plane hitting one of the Trade Towers and said, "That's cool." She immediately told him that this was "for real" and that "lots of mommies and daddies died in the fire." At the point the child burst into tears and became hysterical.

Puncturing children's denial of the awfulness of events may flood them with painful emotions they are not ready to handle. Take your cue from your children, and wait for a time when they are ready to deal with their feelings more directly.

Give your children some slack. Children often show their upset feelings by becoming irritable, fearful, having trouble sleeping, fighting with siblings, or bursting into tears at the slightest frustration. These behaviors may continue for weeks. It's important to keep this in mind, so that instead of saying, "What on earth has gotten into you," when your eight-year-old bursts into tears because his jacket zipper is stuck, you can say, "I can see you are really upset. Maybe you're still thinking about the terrible things that happened. I still feel badly about them, too."

Don't be surprised if your children become fearful about everyday activities. Children may react to hearing about tragedy by worrying about going to school or about seeing their parents go to work. If you encourage them to talk about why they are afraid to go to school or to have you go to work, you may get some clue to what they are really worried about. One seven-year-old who became hysterical when his father left for work insisted that his office building was going to fall down. A five-year-old who couldn't sleep finally got under his bed, "so the ceiling can't land on me." These expressions of fears are opportunities to reassure your child that it is normal to feel upset and worried when something so terrible has happened, but that everything is OK now.

Make yourself more available than usual. One of the most helpful things you can do to help your children cope with the news of a disaster is to spend as much time as possible with them. Children always feel safest in their parents' presence. And the more comfortable and secure they feel, the better able they will be to bring up concerns and questions.

Helping children cope with tragedies and disasters

- Minimize their exposure to radio and television coverage of the disaster.
- Do not overwhelm them with information.
- Follow their lead about how much more they are ready to hear.
- Let them come to grips with the news on their own timetable.
- Let them know you are affected by the tragedy, while at the same time showing you are optimistic about the future.
- Try not to use tragedy as an object lesson about the world.
- Don't interfere with your children's coping mechanisms.
- Give your children some slack.
- If your children become fearful about everyday activities, encourage them to talk about why they are afraid.
- Reassure your children that it is normal to feel upset and worried when something so terrible has happened, but that everything is OK now.
- Make yourself more available than usual.

Should I check up on my thirteen-year-old's party plans?

Q My thirteen-year-old son is very popular and gets invited to many parties. To what extent should I be checking up on the party arrangements by calling the parents ahead of time? A friend of mine told me her daughter went to a party where the parents weren't home and alcohol was available—she only found out from another mom who dropped in early to pick up her daughter. My son seems like a pretty solid citizen, but I do have questions about some of his friends. I hate to start acting like the CIA and dropping in or calling parents ahead of time to see if they will be there, but on the other hand I don't want to be too laid back and discover later that my son is in trouble. How much vigilance is warranted here?

A Regardless of how much you trust your son, it is a good idea to call the parents hosting the party to make sure they will be home. Your son could go to a party thinking parents will be there only to discover they are not and his friends are doing things that make him uncomfortable. Or perhaps he has been told the host's parents will not be there but is unwilling to tell you because he doesn't want to blow the whistle on a friend. The worst scenario is that your son knows there will be no chaperones and plans to use alcohol or drugs. Whatever the case, by making clear to your son that you will always call the party-giver's parents, you protect him from unsafe and illegal activities. And, no matter how much he protests, you demonstrate your love and concern for him.

One footnote: There are some instances when the host's parents are home but the parents allow underage drinking—or even drug use—in the false belief that kids will engage in these activities anyway and it is better if they do it at home under parental supervision. So if you don't know the parents well, when you call to make sure they will be home, it is also a good idea to say something like, "I assume you will make sure that there is no drinking or drug use during the party."

Responding to "I'm fat!"

Q What is the proper response when a daughter says, "I'm fat!" My ten-year-old isn't really fat, but she does have more of a tummy than her skinny friends do.

A We suggest you begin by asking her why she thinks she's fat. It makes a difference whether this is a conclusion she has come to on her own or whether other children are teasing her or comparing her unfavorably to children her age.

If your daughter has decided for herself that she is too heavy, you have an excellent opportunity to explain to her that just as people have different color hair, skin and eyes, they have different bodies. She may be larger boned or naturally more muscular than her friends, or perhaps she is approaching puberty more quickly than they are, which could also cause her to gain weight.

If you haven't spoken with her about the changes her body will go through as she matures, the time has come! Most important is to keep in mind that your opinion means the world to her, so it will help if after you explain to her that she has her own unique body type you tell her that in your eyes she is beautiful and "just right."

If your daughter is feeling "fat" because other children are teasing her or making negative remarks about her, you have the chance to talk with her about how intolerant children can be at this age and how much pressure they can apply to children who don't look, dress or talk exactly like everyone else. Tell her that sometimes the things that her peers may pressure her about will be harmless, such as wearing her hair a particular length. At other times, though, peers may put pressure on her to do things that are unhealthy, such as to look thinner than is good for her. Reassure her that you think she looks wonderful, while at the same time you emphasize that you are always available to talk with her about pressures she is getting from her peers.

Finally, it is probably worth pointing out to your daughter that many of the models she sees in magazines and movies are actually too thin, and that sometimes girls can jeopardize their health trying to look like someone who has a different body type or is really underweight. Most important, tell her how happy you are that she is letting you know how she feels and that you hope she will keep sharing her concerns about herself or anyone or anything else.

Index